ACCLAIM FOR RICHARD LEDERER AND HIS ROLLICKING BOOKS

Adventures of a Verbivore

"*Adventures of a Verbivore* should be required reading for all students of English 101, and language lovers in general."
—Barbara Samson Mills, *Baltimore Sun*

"Lederer leads us on joyous forays. . . . He knows how to entertain while educating and is dedicated to the fascinating history of the words we use to communicate—and to the recording of our unintentional and often very funny misspeaks and miswrites. . . ."
—Judyth Rigler, *San Antonio Express-News*

"[*Adventures of a Verbivore* is] for anyone who savors language, enjoys puzzles and word games, is frustrated with learning vocabulary and grammar—or is in danger of forgetting the joy or just the simple fun of language."
—*Kirkus Reviews*

"Fascinating reading! A rollicking romp through the bountiful world of words. . . . I found *Adventures of a Verbivore* to be an eye-opener and never expect to see words in quite the same way. So I can say to word lovers, writers, speakers, and students alike, if you want to enjoy while you learn, get this book. You'll be glad you did."
—Natalie Atkin, *Minneapolis Star Tribune*

The Miracle of Language

"Richard Lederer has done it again—another delightful, witty, and hugely absorbing celebration of the English language. Is there no stopping the man?"

—Bill Bryson, author of *Made in America*

"Wise and engaging. . . . With *The Miracle of Language*, Lederer, America's foremost wag of words, has also become a sage. . . . That is not to say Lederer has abandoned humor—far from it. *Miracle* is filled with many gems."

—*San Diego Union*

"A veritable Cook's Tour of the wonderful English language— from its major highways to its little-known but fascinating by-ways and back roads."

—Don Hauptman, author of *Cruel and Unusual Puns*

"Entertaining and enlightening . . . a delightful and edifying collection."

—*Publishers Weekly*

Crazy English

"Lederer beguiles and bedazzles. . . ."

—*Los Angeles Times*

"For sheer fun, you couldn't find a nicer gift than *Crazy English* by Richard Lederer."

—James J. Kilpatrick

"*Crazy English?* Crazy like a fox, this man Lederer. Ours is a language that reveals its secrets in winks, allusions, sighs, and giggles. Richard Lederer, being a genius, has taken the giggle road. Don't be bothered that you will laugh from the first page of the book to the last—at the end you will be better equipped to convey exactly what you mean, however serious the subject may be."

—Willard Espy

"Lederer shows just how wild and wacky our language is."

—*Chicago Tribune*

"A joyride . . . Lederer celebrates the semantic antics of our language."

—*Boston Herald*

"If I had been given this book to read in high school or college . . . I would have grown up thinking of my own language as a magic moving sea of possibilities and not as a corset for my mind. The final paragraph ought to be read in every English class in the land and the book ought to be set alongside *The Elements of Style* by Strunk and White as an equal classic."

—Robert Fulghum

Other Books by Richard Lederer

Pun and Games
The Write Way (*with Richard Dowis*)
Nothing Risqué, Nothing Gained
Literary Trivia (*with Michael Gilleland*)
Adventures of a Verbivore
More Anguished English
The Miracle of Language
The Play of Words
Crazy English
Get Thee to a Punnery
Anguished English
Basic Verbal Skills (*with Philip Burnham*)

to Breen and She 11/dar, 8/96

FRACTURED
English

A PLEASURY OF
BLOOPERS AND BLUNDERS,
FLUFFS AND FLUBS,
AND GAFFES AND GOOFS

Richard Lederer

Richard Lederer
Author of *Anguished English*

POCKET BOOKS
New York   London   Toronto   Sydney   Tokyo   Singapore

An *Original* Publication of POCKET BOOKS

POCKET BOOKS, a division of Simon & Schuster Inc.
1230 Avenue of the Americas, New York, NY 10020

ISBN: 0-671-00036-5

First Pocket Books trade paperback printing November 1996

10 9 8 7 6 5 4 3 2 1

POCKET and colophon are registered trademarks of
Simon & Schuster Inc.

Cover design by Brigid Pearson
Front cover photo by Timothy Savard/Photoworks
Text design by Stanley S. Drate/Folio Graphics Co.

Printed in the U.S.A.

For
Al and Jan
and
Marty

ACKNOWLEDGMENTS

For the abundance of fractured fluffs and flubs in this book I am indebted to the hundreds of readers and listeners who offered up their collected goofs and gaffes for national exposure. Special thanks to the National Court Reporters Association and American Association for Medical Transcription for their continued kindness in sharing their court and medical transquips.

I am also indebted to two of my books, *Anguished English* and *More Anguished English,* from which I have drawn a small ration of bloopers. Without such a selective dusting off of some of my all-time favorites, several chapters in this book could not have been cobbled.

CONTENTS

INTRODUCTION

*All I need now is a bit of plastic surgery
to regain the normal width of my mouth.*

Welcome to the blunderful world of bloopers, where crimes and misdemeanors against the English language go unpunished but not unpublished.

Some people are bird watchers. I watch word botchers. The result of my blooper snooping has been three anthologies of accidental assaults upon our mother tongue— *Anguished English, More Anguished English,* and now, *Fractured English.*

Between publication of the first two books, six years trooped by, during which I received about 40,000 submissions and culled the 2,000 best. Between the publication of *More Anguished English* and of this book passed three years. The span was shortened because of the growing enthusiasm of response, volume per square year, and quality of the submissions inspired by the earlier books.

I am sometimes asked if I invent any of the bloopers that appear in my collections. My answer is an emphatic "No way!" No way would I violate the code of ethics of the bloopthologist—the collector takes what he or she finds and contrives nothing. No way could I possibly manufacture the complaint composed by a student to his teacher at the end of the year: "I past all my testes. My grade should be hirer." No way could I make up the wiggy headline LEGISLATORS TAX BRAINS TO CUT DEFICIT. No way could I mangle the receptionist's voice-mail advice, "Please leave a message. The doctors are out of the office or else on the phone and me too." These uncut gems are self-evidently genuine, authentic, certified, and unpolished; they have not been manufactured by any professional humorist. And they are far funnier than anything I could fabricate from whole cloth, even with a lunatic fringe.

"Do you spend all day reading newspapers, magazines, essays, and signs?" is another question I am often asked. Again I answer, "No way." Sure, I happen to happen on some items myself, but the vast bulk are sent me by a conspiracy of super duper blooper snoopers all around our globe. Just as a certain kind of person walks through a field with eyes peeled for four-leaf clovers, blooper snoopers trek through newspapers looking for blunders.

Here's a typical submission, this one from a woman in Encino, California. I won't print her name in case she's still working for the same company:

Dear Mr. Lederer:

At my former job, a lot of us employees weren't too happy with the bosses, and there was often a lot of muttering and griping among us. One afternoon, when the bosses had gone to lunch, one of my co-workers came out of his cubicle and burst out, "There's distention among the troops!" I suggested they try some Pepto-Bismol. Then there's my current boss, not exactly what you'd call a rocket scientist. Referring to the crime of the infamous Lorena Bobbitt, she said, "She severed her husband's appendix." Try a little farther south, boss!

Why do my readers and informants so delight in bloopers and boo-boos, fluffs and flubs, and goofs and gaffes? In their article, "The Appeal of Bloopers," humorologists Donald F. and Alleen Pace Nilsen quote Thomas Fuller's dictum that "birds are entangled by their feet and men by their tongues." The Nilsens sagely add, "In both cases, we are entangled by the very things that set us free."

"Blunders and bloopers are genuinely funny," continue the Nilsens, "because they involve the reader or listener in mentally drawing together two scripts—the one that was said and the one that was intended. To qualify, the error has to be far enough away from the original to communicate some other meaning yet close enough that the listener or reader can connect it to the intended meaning."

The humor in bloopers lies, in part, in the listener's awareness of the speaker's vulnerability. It is the very artlessness of linguistic lapses that makes them so endearing and makes us feel superior. We laugh when we see and hear the verbal rugs pulled out from under somebody else. After all, we would never commit such blunders—or would we?

Aside from giving us the kick of hearing someone else screw up, bloopers are entertaining because they reveal hidden connections between words. That is one of the great joys of our English language, which possesses more than three times the number of words of any other vocabulary. We own more than 600,000 words; no one else owns even 200,000. The formula is simple: the more words in a language, the greater the likelihood that collisions will occur and (to mix a metaphor unrepentantly) that the stomach will be detonated into a rolling boil.

As I've strongly advised in my other books, bloopers are best swallowed in small doses. Don't guzzle them, or you may end up in physical and emotional distress. Listen to some people who ignored the warnings I posted in *More Anguished English:*

> Are you trying to get yourself indicted for murder? After reading *More Anguished English* cover to cover, I now better understand the expression "I died laughing." I indeed laughed so hard I lost my breath. Not that its predecessor didn't have the same effect on me, but I'd forgotten how nearly lethal your books were till I howled my way through *More Anguished English.*
> —Cynthia MacGregor, Lantana, Florida

> Here comes the reason for the lawsuit. I went into gales and fits of laughter. I ended up on the floor, supine, in catatonic spasms, split open all 432 sutures . . . and bled to death.
> —Esther Mosher, Norwell, Massachusetts

> I am, at the moment, trying to recover from reading *More Anguished English.* My GP has assured me

that the cracks in my *abominable* region will heal within a few months, and he has successfully managed to reestablish my jaw to its usual position. All I need now is a bit of plastic surgery to regain the normal width of my mouth, which at present has the likeness of a frog who has tried to swallow a dinosaur's egg.

—Hans Lemböl, Denmark

Norman Cousins, the distinguished editor who overcame a debilitating disease through laughter therapy, wrote, "Illness is not a laughing matter. Perhaps it ought to be. Laughter moves your internal organs around. It enhances respiration. It is an igniter of great expectation." Bloopers books invite you to imbibe the healthful elixirlike effects of hearty laughter:

Thanks for your belly laughs, which are worth a thousand Tylenols.

—James J. Scanlon, Providence, Rhode Island

Your books are good medicine, except for the incontinent.

—Ellen Pilgrim, Goleta, California

Even though I can only type with one hand, I feel that I must write to you about my experience with your book, *More Anguished English*. Four weeks ago, I suffered a stroke, and I have some difficulty with my speech. In order to get some practice reading aloud, I chose to read your book to my wife. The effort was a total failure for that purpose because I got to laughing so much that I couldn't pronounce any words at all. However, the effort did wonders for my weakened facial muscles. So much laughing and smiling strengthened those muscles to the point where my smile is no longer so crooked and my drooping face is looking nearly normal again. My disposition has also improved. I highly recommend your book as essential equipment for any stroke rehabilitation facility. Thanks for your help.

—Ronald R. Lund, M.D., Casper, Wyoming

In Navajo Indian culture, there is something called the First Laugh Ceremony. Tradition dictates that each Navajo baby is kept on a cradle board until he or she laughs for the first time. Then the tribe throws a celebration in honor of the child's first laugh, which is considered to mark his or her birth as a social being.

May this book help you celebrate your membership in human society as *Homo guffawus*, the creature who laughs.

If you are a super duper blooper snooper and would like to contribute to my next collection of skewed and skewered sentences, please send your best howlers to richard.lederer@pobox.com, or to:

Richard Lederer
2655 South Sorrell Street
Las Vegas, NV 89102
http://www.pobox.com/~verbivore

I

SCHOOL DAZE

From the Mouths of Babes

A five-year-old girl called a daddy longlegs "a long-legged father."

After Christmas break, a teacher asked her pupils how they spent their holidays. Here is one small boy's view of retirement in a mobile-home park:

We always spent Christmas with Grandma and Grandpa. They used to live here in a big brick house but Grandpa got retarded and they moved to Florida. They live in a place with a lot of retarded people. They live in tin huts. They ride big tricycles. They go to a big building they call a wreck hall. If it was wrecked, it is fixed now.

They play games there and do exercises but they don't do them too good. There is a swimming pool there, and they go there just to stand in the water with their hats on. I guess they don't know how to swim.

My grandma used to make cookies and stuff, but I guess she forgot how. Nobody cooks there. They all go to fast food restaurants called Early Bird. But I didn't eat any birds. I had eggs.

As you ride into the park, there is a doll house with a man sitting in it. He watches all day so they can't get out without him seeing them. They wear name badges with their names on them. I guess they don't know who they are.

My Grandma said Grandpa worked hard all his life and earned retardment. I wish they would move back home, but I guess the man in the doll house won't let them out.

Another view of senior citizenship, "What a Grandmother Is," was written by a third-grade pupil attending the West Alexandra School, in Bellflower, California:

A grandmother is a lady who has no children of her own. She likes other people's little girls. A grandfather is a man grandmother. He goes for walks with the boys and they talk about fishing and tractors and like that.

Grandmothers don't have anything to do except be there. They're old so they shouldn't play hard or run. It is enough if they drive us to the market where pretend horses are and have lots of dimes. Or if they take us for a walk, they should slow down past things like pretty leaves or caterpillars. They should never say, "Hurry up."

Usually they are fat but not too fat to tie your shoes. They wear glasses and funny underwear. They can take their teeth and gums off. When they read to us, they don't skip or mind if it is the same story again.

It is better if they don't typewrite or play cards except with us. They don't have to be smart, only answer questions like "Why do dogs hate cats?" and "How come God isn't married?"

Everybody should try to have one, especially if you don't have television, because grandmothers are the only grownups who have got time.

The pearls of wit and wisdom—and whiz and witdom—that fall from the mouths of babes are the most charming and innocent bloopers I receive from my readers. I view these "kiddisms" as bloopers-in-training and am confident that when the boys and girls grow up, many will unknowingly contribute more sophisticated and loopy goofs to my books. Here's a selection of embryonic bloopers, written and spoken by elementary-school pupils:

▶ A teacher and her kindergarten students were studying mammals. During lunch, one little boy asked, "Miss Cindy, are we considered mammals?"

"Why yes, Johnny, we are mammals."

One little girl added, "But aren't some of us fe-mammals?"

▶ A woman approached a new student at an elementary school and introduced herself, saying, "Hello, I'm the principal here."

"No, you're not," replied the little girl. "You're the princessipal!"

▶ At Disney World, a four-year-old told his mother, "Goofy is the coldest planet in the solar system." Naturally, he meant Pluto.

▶ At an airport, a 10-year-old boy asked his mother, "Why aren't helicopters called heavencopters? After all, they do rise upward."

▶ A five-year-old girl called a daddy-longlegs "a long-legged father."

▶ Conversation overheard between two little boys:
  "Are you in adultsense now?"
  "No, I think I'm still in Pooh-Bear-ty."

▶ A fifth-grade teacher told her students that members of her profession in the 1800s dressed in ankle-length skirts and long-sleeved blouses, even in summertime. She went on to explain that such garb was necessary because teachers were not allowed to expose their arms or legs.
  A boy piped up from the back of the room: "Oh no, that can't be true. The Constitution gave everyone the right to bare arms."

▶ A little boy accompanied his parents to church for the first time one Sunday morning. After the service, the parents asked their son if he had enjoyed it. "The music was great," said the boy, "but they really should make the commercials shorter."
  During an especially trying time in the classroom, a teacher shrugged her shoulders and sighed, "C'est la vie." The pupils all shouted, "La vie!"

▶ A woman asked a little boy how old he was. "I'm four," said the boy.
  "And when will you be five?"
  "When I'm done being four."

▶ Conversation overheard between another pair of boys:

"Look at all the penises on the cow!"

"Those aren't penises. Those are gutters!"

▶ A six-year-old told his baby-sitter, "We're watching the story of E.T., the Extra Cholesterol."

▶ A sixth-grade boy identified the six New England states as "Maine, Vermont, New Hampshire, Rhode Island, and Massatushy."

▶ An eight-year-old boy, on seeing a beautiful neighbor dressed in a scanty bathing suit, exclaimed, "Mom, come see Linda. She's in a new zucchini!"

▶ To teacher's question, "What is the golden rule?," a little boy responded, "When someone hits you, you hit him back."

▶ "My sister got married, and I was the ringmaster. I got to go to the wedding, but not the conception."

▶ "Auntie, the gray in your hair makes you look very extinguished."

▶ After a mother washed, conditioned, and blow-dried her three-year-old daughter's hair, the little girl thanked her for "air-conditioning my hair."

▶ A four-year-old boy answered the telephone this way: "My sister can't come to the phone. She's upstairs writing in her diarrhea."

▶ After a teacher described the symptoms that had kept her out of school for a week, one of her students suggested, "Gee, maybe you should get an autopsy."

"The child is father of the man," wrote the poet William Wordsworth. Children grow up and become junior-high and high-school students and, ultimately adults and adultresses. To find out what escapes from their mouths, their pens, and their computer keyboards, read on.

Losing the Human Race

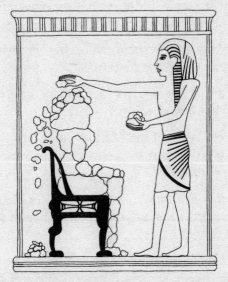

Rosetta Stone was the first queen of Egypt.

A student once proclaimed in a history essay, "History is a never-ending thing."

Another student wrote, "We have plenty of history today because the presidents keep adding to it."

The tricks that students through the ages have played on the chronicles of history is a never-ending source of laughter:

▶ The Egyptians worshiped the god Onassis. They raped mummies in bandages. Rosetta Stone was the first queen of Egypt.

► The Greeks didn't like flappy or fat bodies.

► After the second invasion of Greece, the Athenians took refuse on their ships.

► The Norman invasion was when King Harold owned England, but Norm wanted it.

► Life during the Middle Ages was especially difficult for the pheasants.

► The orders of brothers were the Franciscans, the Dominicans, and the Cisterns.

► The Spanish Inquisition tortured people with tongs and red hot brassieres.

► The chief clause of the Magna Carta was that no free man should be put to death or imprisoned without his own consent.

► The term *Renaissance* refers to the after-birth of learning. During the Renaissance, people began to think for the first time.

► Michelangelo illustrated the Sixteenth Chapter of the book *The Agony and the Ecstasy*. We don't know who did the other fifteen, but they say it was one of the Teenage Mutant Ninja Turtles.

► My favorite character in English history is Henry VIII because he had eight wives and killed them all. Henry VIII lived in a two Door castle. During his reign, the head of the church fell into the hands of the King. Henry VIII thought so much of Wolsey that he made him a cardigan.

► A popular form of entertainment in the 15th century was traveling menstrals.

► Martin Luther is famous for nailing 95 Feces to the

door of the church in Wittenburg. He ate a diet of worms and died.

▶ Unfortunately, Marie Ann Twinette was beheaded. After she died, she had very little chance to continue her career. During the French Revolution, many French nobles requested giblets rather than the guillotine.

▶ Mexico was conquered by Kotex.

▶ "I think, therefore I am" was said by the philosopher Day Cart.

▶ Karl Marx declared that religion was the opinion of the people.

▶ Then there was the Victorian Age, when nice ladies were considered virgins. In that day in time, when people conversated, they conversated proper and with good grammer. In yesteryear, sex was considered sacred and only attempted after marriage. Women wore a lot of accessories in the Victorian age, such as griddles.

Surely, our budding scholars must have a firmer grasp of American history. Surely:

▶ The *Mayflower Compact* was a small ship that brought Columbus to America. Columbus knelt down, thanked God, and put the American flag in the ground. Tarzan is a short name for the American flag. Its full name is Tarzan Stripes.

▶ The French settlement in North America consisted of a series of military fornication up and down the Ohio River.

▶ America was founded by four fathers. The Declaration of Independence says all men are cremated equal and are well-endowed by their creator. The Constitution of the United States was adopted to secure domestic hostility. The first amendment to the Constitution gives me the right to bare arms.

▶ Benjamin Franklin got married and discovered electricity. When he went to the French court, he did not dress. They respected him.

▶ George Washington was a very social man. He had big balls and everyone enjoyed them.

▶ General Burgundy surrendered to Sara's Toga.

▶ Two hardships of the Civil War were the *Monitor* and the *Merrimack*.

▶ Abraham Lincoln lived at the Gettysburg Address. He wrote the exclamation proclamation. His pictures make him look thin and emancipated. Lincoln debated Kennedy on TV in 1960. Kennedy won because he looked good. Lincoln had pallor due to his assassination.

▶ During the early part of World War I, President Wilson urged people to stay in neutral. In the War, the unfortunate soldiers spent day after day up to their wastes in filth.

▶ The New Deal tried to make sure that the stock market will never happen again.

▶ One of the major events of the twentieth Century was World War I, which made people so sad that it brought on something called the Great Depression. World War II happened when Hitler and the Knotsies had erotic dreams of conquest all over Europe, but Franklin Roosevelt went over there and put a stop to him. Hitler committed suicide in his bunk. World War II ended on VD Day.

► Martin Luther was born in Germany and had a dream. He went to Washington and told his Sermon on the Monument. Later, he nailed 96 Protestants in the Watergate scandal, which made a new religious and rasial morality in the United States.

Science Friction

*Dinosaurs became extinct after the flood because
they were too big to get into the ark.*

A student in science class wrote, "The universe is a
giant orgasm." At the end of the student's essay, the
teacher riposted, "Your answer gives new meaning to the
Big Bang Theory."

"Scientists are hypothetical people," wrote a student
of chemistry. The following student comments about science were gleaned from essays, examinations, and classroom discussions. These beguiling theories are in no way
hypothetical. They are all real and attest to the high level
of scientific literacy in our nation:

▶ The three types of rocks are ignacious, metaphoric, and sedentary.

▶ In some rocks we find the fossil footprints of fishes.

▶ Many dead animals of the past changed to fossils while other preferred to be oil.

▶ All animals were here before mankind. The animals lived peacefully until mankind came along and made roads, houses, hotels, and condoms.

▶ Sir Isaac Newton invented gravity.

▶ The law of gravity says no fair jumping up without coming back down.

▶ While the earth seems to be knowingly keeping its distance from the sun, it is really only centrificating.

▶ Galileo showed that the earth was round and not vice versa. He dropped his balls to prove gravity.

▶ Marie and Perrier Curie shared the Noble Prize.

▶ Marie Curie did her research at the Sore Buns Institute in France.

▶ Next week we will experience the venereal equinox.

▶ Proteins are composed of a mean old acid.

▶ The largest mammals are to be found in the sea because there is nowhere else to put them.

▶ Involuntary muscles are not as willing as voluntary ones.

▶ Methane, a greenhouse gas, comes from the burning of trees and cows.

▶ Paraffin is the next order of angels above serrafin.

▶ The ozone level is breaking down more rapidly today because of all our aresoles.

▶ Water is melted steam.

▶ Mushrooms always grow in damp places and so they look like umbrellas.

▶ A monkey has a reprehensible tail.

▶ Some people say we condescended from apes.

▶ The leopard has black spots which look like round soars on its body. Those who catch soars get leprosy.

▶ A cuckoo does not lay its own eggs.

▶ Dinosaurs became extinct after the flood because they were too big to get into the ark.

▶ In spring the salmon swim upstream to spoon.

▶ CO_2 is lighter than air because leaves absorb it, and they are on top of trees.

▶ To remove air from a flask, fill the flask with water, tip the water out, and put the cork in, quick.

▶ The three cavities of the body are the head cavity, the tooth cavity, and the abominable cavity.

▶ The spinal column is a long bunch of bones. The head sits on the top and you sit on the bottom.

▶ Most books say the sun is a star. But it still knows how to change back into the sun in the daytime.

▶ Cadavers are dead bodies that have donated themselves to science. This procedure is called gross anatomy.

▶ The cause of dew is through the earth revolving on its own axis and perspiring freely.

▶ Hot lather comes from volcanoes, and when it cools, it turns into rocks.

▶ A liter is a nest of young baby animals.

▶ The earth makes a resolution every 24 hours.

▶ Parallel lines never meet unless you bend one or both of them.

▶ Algebra was the wife of Euclid.

▶ A circle is a figure with no corners and only one side.

▶ A right angle is 90 degrees Farenhight.

▶ Genetics explains why you look like your father and if you don't, why you should.

▶ A supersaturated solution is one that holds more than it can hold.

▶ In making water, it takes everything from H to O.

▶ Respiration is composed of two acts, first inspiration, and then expectoration.

▶ An example of animal breeding is the farmer who mated a bull that gave a great deal of milk with a bull with good meat.

▶ The hydra gets its food by descending upon its prey and pushing it into its mouth with its testacles.

▶ If conditions are not favorable, bacteria go into a period of adolescence.

▶ The formula for sea water is CH_2O.

▶ Water is composed of two gins, Oxygin and Hydrogin. Oxygin is pure gin. Hydrogin is gin and water.

▶ When oxygen combines with anything, heat is given off. This is known as constipation.

▶ The hookworm larva enters the body through the soul.

▶ As the rain forests in the Amazon are shrinking, so are the Indians.

▶ A major discovery was made by Mary Leaky, who found a circle of rocks that broke wind.

▶ The skeleton is what is left after the insides have been taken out and the outsides have been taken off. The purpose of the skeleton is something to hitch meat to.

▶ You can listen to thunder after lightning and tell how close you came to getting hit. If you don't hear it, you got hit, so never mind.

▶ The Dutch people used windmills to keep the plants from sweating.

▶ Most of the houses in France are made of plaster of Paris.

A class of eighth-graders was asked to write about the pros and cons of marijuana. One student responded: "The pros are the people who sell it. The cons are the people who get caught and land in jail."

Wrote another middle-schooler: "One way to contact AIDS is through annual intercourse. To avoid getting AIDS, men should wear condoms at all times."

Other classics from hygiene classes include:

▶ The union of the egg and sperm is called deception.

▶ Human beings share a need for food, shelter, and sex with lower animals.

▶ People who squeeze their spinster muscles too tight will get constipation.

▶ It is in the virginia that the period of gestication is passed.

▶ Women are reproducing too fast for mankind to keep up.

▶ How is a child's sex determined? The male carries it in his jeans.

▶ The safest sex is absence.

▶ On a date, a boy tries to show how masculine he is. On this point, a girl can help greatly.

▶ Teenage suicide is a problem because approximately 400,000 teenagers attempt to commit suicide and only 7,000 succeed.

▶ In medical studies, some subjects receive medicine while the rest are given placentas.

▶ After somebody dies, their body becomes rigorous.

Finally, here are some science daffynitions concocted by our students, who are well on their way to becoming the scientists of tomorrow:

▶ *Aorta:* a man who makes long speeches.

▶ *Asexual:* reproductions through a disinterested party.

▶ *Canal:* a small stream of water made by man.

▶ *Circle:* a line which meets its other end without ending.

▶ *Cloud:* a high flying fog.

▶ *Equator:* a managerie lion running around the Earth through Africa.

▶ *Germinate:* to become a naturalized German.

▶ *Geyser:* a piece of floating ice that sometimes reaches a boiling point.

▶ *Magnet:* something you find crawling all over a dead cat.

▶ *Migration:* the headache birds get when flying south.

▶ *Momentum:* what you give a person when they are going away.

▶ *One horsepower:* the amount of energy it takes to drag a horse 500 feet in one second.

▶ *Planet:* a body of earth surrounded by sky.

▶ *Quartz:* the name for two pints.

▶ *Rabies:* Jewish priests; must be treated with respect.

▶ *Rhubarb:* a kind of celery gone bloodshot.

▶ *Sound:* a rapid series of osculations.

▶ *Thermometer:* an instrument for raising temperance.

▶ *Vacuum:* a large, empty space where the Pope lives.

▶ *Volcano:* a hole in the ground that gives off molt and lava.

Stop the Music!

The main trouble with a French horn is it's too tangled up.

▶ In the last scene of *Pagliacci,* Canio stabs Neda, who is the one he really loves. Pretty soon, Silvio gets stabbed also and they all live happily ever after.

▶ Caruso was the first Italian. Then someone heard his voice and said he would go a long way. And so he came to America.

▶ Stradivarius sold his violins on the open market with no strings attached.

▶ The principle singer of the 19th-century opera was called pre-Madonna.

▶ At one time, singers had to use musicians to accompany them. Since synthesizers came along, singers can now play with themselves.

▶ All female parts were sung by castrati. We don't know exactly what they sounded like because there are no known descendants.

When it comes to writing about classical music, students across our nation show themselves to be fit as fiddles. They pull out all the stops and never soft-pedal the facts about our musical heritage. Without blowing their own horns, chiming in, or harping on the subject, they strike a responsive chord.

Young scholars have expressed their rapture for the *Bronze Lullaby*, the *Taco Bell Cannon*, Beethoven's *Erotica*, Tchaikovsky's *Cracknutter Suite*, and Gershwin's *Rap City in Blue*. In defining musical terms, they also demonstrate that they know their brass from their oboe:

▶ Music sung by two people at the same time is called a duel. If they sing without music, it is called Acapulco.

▶ A virtuoso is a musician with real high morals.

▶ Contralto is a low sort of music that only ladies sing.

▶ Diatonic is a low-calorie Schwepps.

▶ Probably the most marvelous fugue was the one between the Hatfields and the McCoys.

▶ A harp is a nude piano.

▶ An oboe is an American tramp. (written by a British student)

▶ A Stradivarius is a prehistoric animal.

▶ My favorite instrument is the bassoon. It is so hard to

play, people seldom play it. That is why I like the bassoon best.

▶ The main trouble with a French horn is it's too tangled up.

▶ An opera is a song of bigly size.

▶ An interval in music is the distance from one piano to the next.

▶ The correct way to find the key to a piece of music is to use a pitchfork.

▶ *Agitato* is a state of mind when one's finger slips in the middle of playing a piece.

▶ *Refrain* means don't do it. A refrain in music is the part you'd better not try to sing.

▶ I know what a sextet is, but I'd rather not say.

Students sing a different tune and play it by ear when they write about the famous composers, even those who never existed:

▶ Most authorities agree that music of antiquity was written long ago. My favorite composer was opus. Agnus Dei was a woman composer famous for her church music.

▶ Henry Purcell was a well-known composer few people have ever heard of.

▶ Johann Sebastian Bach wrote a great many musical compositions and had a large number of children. In between, he practiced on an old spinster which he kept up in his attic. Bach died from 1750 to the present.

► Bach was the most famous composer in the world and so was Handel. Handel was half German, half Italian, and half English. He was very large.

► Beethoven wrote three symphonies: the Third, the Fifth, and the Ninth. He wrote music even though he was deaf. Beethoven was so deaf he wrote loud music. He took long walks in the forest even when everyone was calling him. I guess he could not hear so good. Beethoven expired in 1827 and later died for this. Do you know that if Beethoven were alive today, he would be celebrating the 165th anniversary of his death?

► Rock Mananoff was a famous post-Romantic composer of piano concerti.

► Aaron Copland is one of our most famous contemporary composers. It is unusual to be contemporary. Most composers do not live until they are dead.

The Revised
Nonstandard Bible

The Virg 'n' Mary

A Sunday-school teacher was talking about Christmas and the coming of Christ and she asked, "And what was Jesus' mother's name?"

"Mary," all said.

"Now what was his father's name?"

One little fellow raised his hand. "Virg."

"Virg? Where did you get that idea?"

"Well," answered the boy, "they always talk about the Virg 'n' Mary!"

Another religion teacher was telling her class the story of Lot. "Lot was warned to take his wife and flee out of the city, but his wife looked back and she was turned to salt." She looked around the class, and one little girl tentatively raised her hand. "Yes?" said the teacher.

"I was wondering," said the girl, "what happened to the flea?"

When a Hebrew school teacher intoned, "The Lord Our God is one," little Benjamin asked, "When will he be two?"

An art teacher in a Maine elementary school also taught Sunday school, where she had the little ones draw pictures of the Bible stories. Little Emma proudly presented her picture of the journey to Bethlehem. The drawing showed an airplane flying over the desert. In the passenger area were seated Joseph and Mary and little Jesus.

"The drawing is fine," said the teacher, "but who's that up front flying the plane?"

Answered Emma, "Why, that's Pontius the Pilot."

Another religion teacher told her first-graders to draw a big picture of the story of Adam and Eve and the garden of Eden. One little boy drew a big car with God at the wheel, driving Adam and Eve out of Paradise.

When yet another teacher asked her student why there was a dog in the nativity drawing, the fledging artist explained that it was a German shepherd. That dog has been joined in the gallery of Sunday-school portraiture by a grinning bear with crossed eyes—Gladly, the Cross-Eyed Bear, of course.

Sunday-school boys and girls not only produce graphic misinterpretations of the Bible in their drawings, they also rewrite biblical history with amazing grace. It is truly astonishing what happens to Bible stories when they are retold by young scholars around the world:

The Bible is full of many interesting caricatures. Michael Angelo painted them on the Sixteen Chapels.

The first five books of the Bible are Genesis, Exodus, Laxatives, Deuteronomy, and Numbers. In the first book of the Bible, Guinessis, God got tired of creating the world, so he took the Sabbath off. Adam and Eve were created from an apple tree. One of their children, Cain, asked, "Am I my brother's son? My punishment is greater than I can bare."

Noah's wife was called Joan of Ark. He built an ark, which the animals came on to in pears. Lot's wife was a pillar of salt by day but a ball of fire by night. Saddam and Gomorrah were twins.

Abraham begat Isaac and Isaac begat Jacob and Jacob begat 12 partridges. God asked Abraham to sacrifice Isaac on Mount Montezuma. Abraham took Isaac up the mountain to be circumcised. Jacob, son of Isaac, stole his brother Esau's birthmark. Esau was a man who wrote fables and sold his copyright for a mess of potash. Jacob was a patriarch who brought up his 12 sons to be patriarchs, but they did not take to it. One of Jacob's sons, Joseph, gave refuse to the Israelites.

The Jews were a proud people and throughout history they had trouble with the unsympathetic Genitals. Samson was a strongman who let himself be led astray by a Jezebel like Delilah. Samson slayed the Philistines with the axe of the apostles. He slayed them by pulling down the pillows of the temple.

Pharaoh forced the Hebrew slaves to make beds without straw. Moses was an Egyptian who lived in a hark made of bullrushes. Moses led the Hebrews to the Red Sea, where they made unleavened bread, which is bread made without any ingredients. The Egyptians were all drowned in the dessert.

Afterwards, Moses went up on Mount Cyanide to get the Ten Amendments. The First Commandment was when Eve told Adam to eat the apple. The Fifth Commandment is humor thy father and mother. The Seventh Commandment is thou shalt not admit adultery. The Ninth Commandment is thou salt not bare faults witness.

Moses ate nothing but whales and manner for 40 years. He died before he ever reached Canada. Then, Joshua led the Hebrews in the battle of Geritol. The greatest miracle in the Bible is when Joshua told his son to stand still and he obeyed him.

David was a Hebrew king skilled at playing the liar. He wrote psalms. They are called psalms because he sang them while playing the harmonica. David also fought with the Finkelsteins, a race of people who lived in Biblical times. Solomon, one of David's sons, had 300 wives and 700 porcupines.

Later came Job, who had one trouble after another. Eventually, he lost all his cattle and all his children and had to go live alone with his wife in the desert. Then came Shadrach, Meshach, and To Bed We Go, and then Salome, who was a wicked woman who wore very few clothes and took them off when she danced before Harrods.

When Mary heard that she was the Mother of Jesus, she sang the Magna Carta. When the three wise guys from the East Side arrived, they found Jesus in the manager wrapped in waddling clothes. In the Gospel of Luke they named him Enamel. Jesus was born because Mary had an immaculate contraption. St. John, the Blacksmith, dumped water on his head.

Jesus wrote the "B" Attitudes and enunciated the Golden Rule, which says to do one to others before they do one to you. He also explained, "Man doth not live by sweat alone." Jesus was crucified on his way to Calgary. It was a miracle when he rose from the dead and managed to get the tomb stone off the entrance.

The people who followed the Lord were called the 12 decibels. The epistles were the wives of the apostles. One of the opossums was St. Matthew, who was by profession a taximan.

St. Paul cavorted to Christianity. He preached holy acrimony, which is another name for marriage. A Christian should have only one wife. This is called monotony. The natives of Macedonia did not believe in Paul, so he got stoned.

Other Christians were condemned to death in large groups. They entered the arena to face wild lions, singing hymns of praise in the name of the Father, the Son, and In-the-Hole-He-Goes. The Romans went to the coliseum to watch the Christians die for the fun of it. But, as Mel Brooks says, "The meek shall inherit the earth."

Pullet Surprising Literature

*His father was Mr. Shakespeare and
his mother was Mrs. Shakespeare.*

On a test, an English teacher in Chickasha, Oklahoma,
asked her students, "What distinguished writing award
did Harper Lee win for her novel, *To Kill a Mockingbird?*"
One student wrote, "Harper Lee won a Pullet Surprise."

Each of the following student bloopers is indeed wor-
thy of a pullet surprise. Only in the classroom can you
discover that Victor Hugo wrote *Lame Is Rob* and that
another famous French writer, Emily Zola, penned a famous letter entitled *J'acuzzi.*

Leave it to our young scholars to inform us that Albert

Campus authored *The Plaque* and that Robert Browning shows his lighter side in "The Pied Piper of Hamlet." American lit is relit with the facts that Ernest Hemingway crafted *For Whom the Belt Holds*, that John Steinbeck created *Of My Cement*, that Harper Lee's masterpiece is *Tequilla Mockingbird*, and that J. D. Salinger gave the world *Catch Her in the Rye*. Did you know that Anonymous is the man who writes all the poems that are not signed?

Mount Olympus might erupt with laughter on hearing the way students describe the gods and goddesses. Hera had only one way to control Zeus and viewed sex as a means of coming to an end. The Greek goddess of love was Alpodite. Aphrodite lives on today as a kind of haircut—the Aphro.

Vesta was a goddess who kept the home fries burning. Dionysius was the god of rivalry. Bacchus first taught the Greeks to get drunk. The messenger god was named Herpes, while the god of metalworking was Hepatitus. Persephone was a girl who had an on-and-off relationship with Pluto.

Students render—and rend—classical mythology with unintended, classic humor. Many a young scholar has defined a myth as "a female moth." One myth says that the mother of Achilles dipped him in the River Stynx until he became intolerable. Achilles appears in *The Iliad*, by Homer. Homer also wrote *The Oddity*, in which Penelope is the last hardship that Odysseus endures on his journey.

Odysseus is one of many heroes in ancient iniquity. While Odysseus is off sleeping with goddesses, Penelope has to stay at home and beat off all those suitors. When Odysseus comes home in disguise, his old nurse recognizes him by his scared thigh, which he gets from a wild bore. Odysseus has to sail between Scylla and Charybdis. Being between Scylla and Charybdis means that whichever way you go, you are going to get got.

Sophocles wrote the famous Greek play *Oedipus Wrecks*. Oedipus screws up very badly when he marries his own mother who was really his wife, which the Erkel knew it all along. Oedipus forces out his eyes and condoms himself. Oedipus and Hamlet really had a lot in common, even if Freud had not yet been invented.

The creator of Hamlet was, of course, William Shakespeare. Through their bloopers, many generations of students have gone from bard to verse:

The greatest writer of the Renaissance was William J. Shakespeare. Shakespeare was born in the year 1564, supposedly on his birthday. His father was Mr. Shakespeare, and his mother was Mrs. Shakespeare. He wrote during the era in which he lived. Actually, Shakespeare wasn't written by Shakespeare but by another man named Shakespeare.

Shakespeare never made much money and is famous only because of his plays and sonics. He lived at Windsor with his merry wives, writing hysterectomies, tragedies, comedies, and errors. I don't see why he is so popular when his writing skills are so low. He wrote in Islamic pentameter, and you can't hardly understand what he is saying.

In one of Shakespeare's famous plays, Hamlet rations out his situation by relieving himself in a long soliloquy. A soliloquy is a conversation between one person. Hamlet has an edible complex, and his mind is filled with the filth of incestuous sheets which he pours over every time he sees his mother. Hamlet decides to act madly so he gets in an antic position. In Act Five, Hamlet talks to Horatio about a skull that has been thrown up. Act Five comes right after Act Four.

In another play, Macbeth was from his mother's womb untamely ripped. He is a brave and strong man who turns bad and gradually gets worse.

King Duncan wires Macbeth that he will be spending the night at his castle. Then Lady Macbeth tries to convince Macbeth to kill King Duncan by attacking his manhood. All Macbeth does is follow his wife's odors. He kills the king on page 14. Macbeth and Lady Macbeth then suffer from quilt. In fact, they have so much quilt, they can't sleep at night.

During the banquet scene, Lady Macbeth is afraid her husband will expose himself in front of his guests. Then Lady Macbeth gets kilt. The proof that the witches in *Macbeth* were supernatural is that no one could eat what they cooked.

Romeo and Juliet are an example of a heroic couplet. This story presents a one on one situation between a man and a woman. Romeo and Juliet belonged to the families of the Montages and Copulates. They tell each other how much they are in love in the baloney scene. After much fighting in the pubic square, Romeo's last wish is to be laid by Juliet.

In *Julius Caesar*, Brutus is a tragic hero despite dying at the end. Caesar is murdered by the Ides of March because they think he is going to be made king. Dying, he gasps out the words "Tee hee, Brutus." Then he dies with these immortal words: "Veni, vedi, vici."

In *The Merchant of Venice*, the Rialto is the business part of Venus. Bassanio loved Portia, but he had no money to press his suit. *Taming of the Screw* is a play about Petruchio, who takes Kate from a bitter screw to an obedient wife. The clown in *As You Like It* is named Touch-down. In that play, Shakespeare wrote, "All the world's a stage, and everyone is just acting."

In *Anthony and Cleopatra,* Cleopatra reclined to become Mark Anthony's mistress. She took the Roman Empire one man at a time. The barge she shat on, like a bur-nished throne, glowed on the water. The poop was beaten gold.

Writing at the same time as Shakespeare was Miguel Cervantes. He wrote *Donkey Hote.* The next great author was John Milton. Milton wrote *Paradise Lost.* Then his wife died and he wrote *Paradise Regained.*

From its earliest beginnings to the present day, the canon of English and American literature gets reamed in the classroom:

► Caedmon composed simple hymns in praise of God, using his Germanic tool.

► Several of Herrick's poems use the tradition of *crape diem.* In "To the Virgins, to Make Much of Time," Her-rick warns that if they do not loosen up, they will not have any friends. Being a virgin is OK for people who are old, like teachers and parents, and who do not want to be popular. But this poem is telling us to have some fun now so that we can die with a smile on our face.

► Many of the poems in this selection have a basic theme of death, which was quite common in the times of Romantic literature. Not even the dust of Ozyman-dias' remains remains.

► Edgar Allan Poe was a very curdling writer. He had several additions. One of his additions was alcohol.

Poe was a very sad man. Because he was such a sad man, he wrote very sad stories. The reason he was so sad is that he was impudent. Because he was impudent, he could never love a woman. He could only love little girls. He married a little girl, but he was impudent, so they never had any children.

▶ Mr. Murdstone treated David Copperfield's Mother like a very terranical mail shovenist.

▶ When Arthur Dimmesdale felt guilt about his sin in *The Scarlet Letter,* he felt better when he went on the scaffold and relieved himself.

▶ Henry Wadsworth Longfellow was born in Portland, Maine, while his parents were traveling abroad.

▶ Emily Dickinson was a wreck loose in society.

▶ In *The Mayor of Casterbridge,* when Henchard sold his wife to another man, their marital relationship was not healthy.

▶ Anton Chekhov was the son of Russian pheasants.

▶ In *Of Human Bondage,* Philip stays up all night studding with Mildred.

▶ Suicide was a way of life for Hemingway.

▶ Willie Loman was never more than an average salesman, and people didn't remember him for miles around. Willy Loman's suicide at the end of *Death of a Salesman,* by Author Miller, leads him to think there is a better way of life.

▶ In *A Streetcar Named Desire,* the climax is when Blanche goes to bed with Stella's husband. At the end,

Blanche goes to a mental institution, where she discovers what life is really like.

▶ *Lord of the Flies* is a story about a bunch of boys on an uninhibited desert island.

II

IT'S A
BLUNDERFUL LIFE

Poly-Tickle Speeches

"I don't want to cast asparagus at my opponent!"

During the 1968 Democratic convention in Chicago, crowds of protestors picketed the proceedings and rioted outside the convention center. Longtime Chicago mayor Richard J. Daley ordered police to quell the disruptions and explained to the press, "The police are not here to create disorder. They are here to preserve disorder!"

Mr. Daley was known for beheading the English language with such mutilations as:

▶ I resent your insinuendoes.

▶ No man is an Ireland.

▶ Today the real problem is the future.

▶ We shall reach greater and greater platitudes of achievement.

▶ Don't forget to get out early and vote often.

The mayor's creative word choices must have been contagious, because another Chicago politician was heard to shout, "I don't want to cast asparagus at my opponent!"

Life may get complicated and confused, but leave it to politicians to clear everything up. Or, as a Wisconsin state legislator proclaimed, "Good communication is essential—even if it isn't clear."

"Being in the legislature is no bed of gravy," one of these giants of political thought observed. That was the same Minnesota state senator who said, "Let's dispense with all the discussion and get to the crotch of the matter."

Poet Percy Bysshe Shelley once wrote that "poets are the unacknowledged legislators of the world." Equally true is that politicians are the unacknowledged poets of the world. They can certainly turn a phrase—inside out.

In political debate, the level of language soars to the absolute pinnacle of platitude. When confronted with a charge that the Democrats had "put New York State in a pickle," the Democratic state assembly leader thundered, "We find ourselves in this pickle because you bought that jar and filled it not with pickles but with water, and now you're trying to jam it in the public's face!"

In a nationally televised debate, Walter Mondale stated, "George Bush doesn't have the manhood to apologize."

Bush fired back: "Well, on the manhood thing, I'll put mine up against his any time."

In discussing a local flood, former California Governor Pat Brown observed, "This is the worst disaster in California since I was elected." Here are more executive and legislative platitudes that fill the anals of political science:

► Announced President Bill Clinton, "I believe that this country's policies should be heavily biased in favor of nondiscrimination."

► "We will not close any base that is not needed," proclaimed former Secretary of Defense Les Aspen, more revealingly than he may have known.

► "If we don't make some changes, the status quo will remain the same," said another member of Clinton's staff.

► "We're going to have the best-educated American people in the world," promised former Vice President Dan Quayle, who also proclaimed, "I support efforts to limit the terms of members of Congress, especially members of the House and members of the Senate."

► "If Lincoln were alive today, he'd roll over in his grave," said former President Gerald Ford, at a Lincoln's birthday dinner. Ford also said, "Things are more like they are now than they have ever been."

► Responding to a question on whether she had expected murder convictions for the Branch Davidians on trial, Attorney General Janet Reno said: "I always wait until a jury has spoken before I anticipate what they will do."

► Former Michigan Governor George Romney offered

clarification: "I didn't say that I didn't say it. I said that I didn't say that I said it. I want to make that very clear."

▶ Answering accusations that he failed to pay his taxes, former New York City Mayor David Dinkins reasoned, "I haven't committed a crime. What I did was fail to comply with the law."

▶ We have two incredibly credible witnesses here," announced U.S. Senator Joe Biden at the U.S. Supreme Court confirmation hearings for Clarence Thomas. One of those unbelievably believable witnesses was Thomas, now a justice on the court, who repeatedly denied "*un*categorically" Anita Hill's allegations of sexual harassment.

▶ Argued law-and-order Philadelphia mayor Frank Rizzo, who had also been chief of police, "The streets are safe in Philadelphia. It's only the people who make them unsafe."

▶ When he heard that the indicted Spiro Agnew was asking to have his corruption case tried by the House instead of in a regular court, Rep. Charles Vanik of Ohio exclaimed, "He's trying to take the decision out of the hands of 12 honest men and give it to 435 Congressmen!"

▶ Sen. Wally Horn of Iowa commented on the issue of what size basketball girls should use: "Girls shouldn't play with men's balls. Their hands are too small."

▶ "Sure, it's going to kill a lot of people, but they may be dying of something else anyway," reasoned a member of the Texas pesticide review board, on chlordane.

► "The exports include thumbscrews and cattle prods, just routine items for the police," stated a Commerce Department spokesman on a regulation allowing the export of various products abroad.

► Lawrence Summers, chief economist of the World Bank, explained why we should export toxic wastes to Third World countries: "I've always thought that the underpopulated countries in Africa are vastly underpolluted."

► "That lowdown scoundrel deserves to be kicked to death by a jackass—and I'm just the one to do it!" shouted a congressional candidate in Texas.

► A Louisiana lawmaker, loudly opposing a bill for the benefit of dependent children, shouted, "To hell with posterity. What's posterity ever done for us?" A state representative from Jackson, Louisiana, complained (when opposing an apparently popular measure), "I can't believe that we are going to let a majority of the people decide what's best for this state." Other Louisiana legislators have been recorded as saying, "I don't want to beat a dead horse to death" and "This mortality rate is killing us" and "I am not sure I understand the question, but I agree with you."

► A political candidate confronted by questions from a Philadelphia reporter begged off, saying, "Candidly, I cannot answer that. The question is too suppository."

► "Topless dancing is at the bottom of our problem!" squawked a San Francisco mayor.

► A West Virginia legislator with a pro-life stance, advocating tough anti-abortion legislation, stated that he was opposed to abortion except when necessary to save the life of the mother or the child.

▶ A New Hampshire congressman declared, "What the people of this state deserve is clean, fresh, wholesome pasteurized milk. And I'm going to the State House and take the bull by the horns until we get it."

▶ Explaining why he would never return to Washington, former Defense Secretary Bobby Ray Inman concocted this metaphor: "I came to a fork in the road and I took it."

▶ Reacting to the NFL's pulling the Super Bowl out of Arizona, U.S. Senator Dennis DeConcini riposted, "Those who throw rocks in glass houses had better look at yourself."

▶ Leave it to Washington, D.C. Mayor Marion Barry to say, "Outside of the killings, we have one of the lowest crime rates in the nation."

▶ U.S. Senator Barbara Boxer announced, "Those who survived the San Francisco earthquake said, 'Thank God I'm still alive.' But, of course, those who died, their lives will never be the same again."

▶ When he was governor of New Hampshire, John Sununu mangled a metaphor thusly: "The bankers' pockets are bulging with the sweat of the honest working man."

▶ Former Secretary of the Treasury John Connally explained, "In the early sixties, we were strong, we were virulent."

▶ A New Mexico state senator told the governor, "The ball is in your camp now."

▶ A newly elected justice of the peace in New Mexico, asked to enforce a law prohibiting cohabitation without benefit of marriage, said, "That would be like looking through a needle for a haystack."

▶ "Let's jump off that bridge when we come to it," said a three-time mayor with a 36-year career in politics.

The word *politics* derives from *poly*, "many," and *ticks*, "blood-sucking parasites." Here are more classics of poly-tickle science:

▶ There comes a time when you have to put principle aside and do what's right.

▶ It doesn't pay to fiddle while Rome is burning and the tigers are nipping at our heels. From time to time, you must divorce yourself from the heat of battle, drop back 10, and count your marbles.

▶ Clamping down on illegal aliens is a giant leap down a very dangerous road.

▶ Some of our friends wanted it in the bill, some wanted it out, and Jerry and I are sticking with our friends.

▶ I came out of that session smiling like a rose.

▶ Anyone working for the town should be above and beyond approach.

▶ The worm has turned and the shoe is on the other foot.

▶ We don't want to skim the cream off the crop here.

▶ To be demeanered like that is an exercise in fertility.

▶ I deny the allegations, and I defy the allegators.

- If somebody's gonna stab me in the back, I want to be there.

- When you're talking to me, keep your mouth shut.

- If you forget the complications, it's all very simple.

- It's the sediment of the house that we adjourn.

- Let's do this in one foul swoop.

- In the 1930s, we were not just on our backs. We were prone on our backs.

- I want to thank each and every one of you for having extinguished yourselves in this session.

- We'll run it up the flagpole and see who salutes that booger.

- People planning on having serious accidents should have their seat belts on.

- The poor are wallowing in the midst of the asphalt jungle.

- That bill, if passed, will derail the ship of state.

- This session has been hit by an avalanche of creeping paralysis.

- I would like to take this time to reirritate my remarks.

- The average age of a 7-year-old in this state is 13.

- In 1994, Americans stand on the horns of an enema.

- I hate to confuse myself with the facts.

- We have a permanent plan for the time being.

- Family planning has many misconceptions.

▶ It's time to grab the bull by the tail and look it squarely in the eye.

▶ The people in my district do not want this highway bypass, no matter if it goes through or around the city.

▶ I think I misquoted myself.

▶ My knowledge is no match for his ignorance.

▶ As long as I am in the Senate, there will be a nuclear suppository in our state.

▶ I don't necessarily believe what I think.

▶ I know what I believe is different from what I think.

▶ This body is becoming entirely too laxative about some matters.

▶ These numbers are not my own; they are from someone who knows what he's talking about.

▶ Panama belongs to us. We stole it fair and square.

▶ This year's grant application represents a 360-degree turn from last year.

▶ Do you realize that DNR wants to buy up millions of acres of land in northern Wisconsin that have been untouched by nature?

▶ This bill will help rural Wisconsin and sparsely populated large cities.

▶ This is a good health bill. Take it from one who has survived a terminal heart attack.

▶ My colleague is listening with a forked ear.

▶ Don't rock the trough.

A member of the Michigan House of Representatives noted, "The House will not allow you to circumvent the rules unless you do it right." I don't mean to cast asparagus, but when politicians circumvent the rules of the English language, they certainly do it right.

A Guide to Sportspeak

He threw 100 pitches in six innings, and that's a mouthful.

The Philadelphia Eagles are playing the Miami Dolphins in a televised game. The play-by-play commentator explains that Philadelphia is beginning to contain Miami's explosive offense, but a muscle-brained metaphor bursts through his line: "It appears as though the Achilles' heel of the Eagles' defense is about to rear its ugly head."

Welcome to the wonderful world of sportspeak, where modifiers are mangled, participles dangled, and metaphors mixed with abandon. The broadcast booth is an unremitting font of anguished English. Take (please!) these classic pieces of play-by-play commentary from

Jerry Coleman, for many years the radioman for the San Diego Padres:

▶ There's a long drive! Winfield is going back, back, back! He hits his head against the wall! It's rolling to second base!

▶ Next up is Fernando Gonzales, who is not playing tonight.

▶ The Padres took a three-game series from the Giants, three games to two.

▶ The pitcher has a blister on the index hand of his pitching finger.

The English language and the game of baseball would be immeasurably the poorer without the fractured diction and unruly grammar of St. Louis Cardinals pitcher and broadcaster Dizzy Dean. Dean peppered his commentaries with *ain't*s and double negatives, and when he thought a verb too colorless, he invented his own, as in "He slud into third base" or "The pitcher flang the ball." When an indignant listener complained, "Mr. Dean, don't you know the king's English?" Dizzy reflected for a moment, then replied, "Sure I do—and so's the Queen."

Ever since Dizzy Dean's verbal vagaries, broadcasters have been slaughtering the king's English:

▶ Arnie Palmer, usually a great putter, seems to be having trouble with his long putts. However, he has no trouble dropping his shorts.

▶ He's already got two championship rings under his belt.

► Folks, this is perfect weather for today's game. Not a breath of air.

► We'll be back with the recap, right after this message.

► That long drive actually sailed into the second balcony and hit a fan on the fly.

► Wrigley Field—it sort of reminds you of some of the old ballparks.

► We're coming up on the rubber game of a four-game series.

► Magic Johnson's three field goals have taken the sails out of the crowd.

► He threw a hundred pitches in six innings, and that's a mouthful.

► Listen to that! Eighty thousand football fans, and not one of them is making a sound!

► He ran the punt return back.

► They really miss the absence of Louis Lipps.

► Just don't think that Boston is going to blow up and dry away.

► The playoff picture is very complicated at this point. Let's call on Chris Berman to unweave the tapestry.

"Are you any relation to your brother Marv?" New Jersey Nets guard Leon Wood asked Steve Albert, Nets TV commentator. "I've never had major knee surgery on any other part of my body," observed Winston Bennett, University of Kentucky basketball forward. "You won't find a single four-letter word in my autobiography. I don't go for that bullshit," stated Hall of Fame pitcher Bob Feller.

Not so surprisingly, coaches and managers throw more screwballs than their players. After a close loss to St. Louis in the 1982 World Series, Milwaukee Brewers manager Harvey Kuenn revealed, "I told my players that they had nothing to be ashamed of. They could hang their heads high."

Observed New York Yankees and Mets manager Casey Stengel, "Good pitching always stops good hitting, and vice versa." Go figure.

In an award presentation to Joe DiMaggio, Yogi Berra, a Stengel protégé, gushed, "Joe, I want to thank you for teaching me that the only way to do something correctly is to do it right."

Detroit Tigers manager Sparky Anderson confided, "I've got my faults, but living in the past isn't one of them. There's no future in it." Chicago White Sox skipper Al Lopez fungoed an inadvertent pun when he said to a reporter, "Sievers will be a great insurance policy to us. He can spell Ted Kluszewski at first base." Shortly after being fired, Atlanta Braves manager Russ Nixon sighed, "I feel I did everything I could do, and probably more."

Let's not pick on the national pastime. "Football is an incredible game," proclaimed long-time Dallas Cowboys coach Tom Landry. "Sometimes it's so incredible, it's unbelievable."

Some pigskin pronouncements are so incredible, they're unbelievable. When he said, "We keep beating ourselves, but we're getting better at it," former Buffalo Bills coach Hank Bullough showed that football coaches can keep up with their counterparts in baseball. Cleveland Browns coach Sam Rutigliano blocked a metaphor as he explained why his team lost: "If you can't make the putts and can't get the man in from second in the bottom of the ninth, you're not going to win enough football games in this league."

The late Bill Peterson, who helped develop some of the nation's outstanding football coaches while building Florida State University into a national football power, was as famous for his loopy language as for his coaching abilities:

▶ I'm the football coach around here and don't you remember it.

▶ The greatest thing just happened to me. I got indicted into the Florida Sports Hall of Fame. They gave me a standing observation.

▶ You guys have to run a little more than full speed out there.

▶ You guys line up alphabetically by height.

▶ You guys pair off in groups of threes, then line up in a circle.

▶ We're not going to be a three-clouds-and-a-yard-of-dust kind of team.

Other coaches and managers manage the English language incorrectly to the point of doing it wrong. Toronto Maple Leafs coach Frank Smith announced, "I have nothing to say, and I'm going to say it just once." An unidentified NBA coach malapropped, "At some point, the team has to be held to account if there are too many fragrant fouls."

A college football coach commented on the prospects for next season: "Well, I'd say our greatest weakness is our lack of strength. Of course, I think you'll see some improvement as we get better."

Noted another coach: "We've got a lot of talent here, but we obviously need a lot of shoring up in several positions depthwise. This year we have to do a lot of weeding out and see what cream comes to the top."

Added a third: "If they ever take the emotion out of football, the stadiums will be full of no-shows."

"I blew it the way I saw it," confessed Ralph DeLeonardis, a minor-league baseball umpire, on a disputed call. That's how sportspeak works. You blow it the way you say it—and the cream comes to the top.

Blessed Bloopers

Kerry Bengston is a 10-ear member of the church.

A minister was scheduled to address a luncheon club. During the meal, the frustrated program chairperson bustled up to advise, "Something's gone wrong with the sound system. You'll have to speak up, preacher. The agnostics in this room are just terrible."

Even in the sanctuary of the church, ministers and priests can make some unholy mistakes in their sermons. Thundered one minister, "We should be as much concerned about those in spiritual danger as those in physical danger. If I were driving through town and saw that Mrs. Smith here had fallen into a canal, I wouldn't drive on and leave her there. I would stop the car, jump into the water, pull her out, and immediately begin giving her artificial insemination."

Another preacher informed his congregation, "One person who especially needs our prayers is Mrs. Jones. It appears that amputation will be necessary. In fact, gonorrhea has already set in."

Yet another minister explained: "This is my second sermon on sin. Last week's point sermon emphasized six points and went overtime, so today's sermon on sin will be pointless."

A pastor in Alabama reminded his flock, "Please don't let anything prevent you from missing this wonderful picnic."

Reading the morning scripture, a priest intoned, "Greater love hath no man than this, that he lay down his wife for his friend."

Another cleric offered this final benediction: "May all your desires be fulfilled, especially your deep desire for onion with God."

Here are some more sanctimonious slips, these from the pages of church bulletins, signs, and orders of service. I offer these, in the words of Sarah, in the book of Genesis, "so that all that hear will laugh with me." As Job said, they "fill my mouth with laughing, and thy lips with rejoicing":

▶ Support our church rummage sale: a good opportunity to get rid of anything not worth keeping but too good to throw away. Bring your husband.

▶ Please bring nonparishable foods to the church tonight.

▶ A bean supper will be held Saturday evening in the church basement. Music will follow.

► The choir of the Church of the Enunciation will perform in the upcoming choir festival.

► The rosebud on the altar this morning is to announce the birth of David Alan Beiser, the sin of Rev. and Mrs. Julius Beiser.

► Low self-esteem support group. 7–8:30 P.M. Eastview Baptist Church. Please use the back door.

► Today will be a Called Council Meeting fight after the church service. Come and vote!

► In November, Mr. Larkin passed out and explained the Finance Committee's budget forms for the 1994–95 church year.

► Monday, 11:30 A.M. to 8:30 P.M. Rain or shine. Pancake luncheon and supper under the auspices of the Sisterhood. All the pancakes you can eat!

Thursday, 7:45 P.M. Choir rehearsal. There will be no meeting of the Sisterhood this month on account of the Pancake luncheon and supper.

► Women in Harmony makes its debut at the Immanuel Baptist Church in Portland next week. The chorus's repertoire is clearly woman-centered, but doesn't lack broad-based appeal.

► Among the topics to be discussed by the church women's group will be abortion, family life, and youth in Asia.

► A massage by the Rev. Mr. Stuart, of the Pilgrim Holiness Church, will follow the singing.

► Fall Apple Pie Sale—Made from the ladies of the church.

▶ Sunday Evening Summer Program

   Begins June 11, 6:00–7:30

   Family Whorship Service

▶ The choir will sing "I Am But a Small Vice."

▶ We are happy to announce that we have secured the services of Rev. Struthers as our organist and choir-master. He will also help with the youth club. We could not get a better man.

▶ Sermon: Come Onto Me

▶ The hymen for today is . . .

▶ A new worship service especially for the community. Don't dress up and come to the gym! 10:20–11:30 A.M. Sundays.

▶ In a church parking lot:
   CHURCH PARKING ONLY
   VIOLATORS TO WED
   AT THEIR OWN EXPENSE

▶ Signs on a church:
   TRUST IN GOD / HAVE FAITH IN THE LORD
   SECURITY BY FRANKLIN BURGLAR ALARM, INC.

▶ Kerry Bengston is a 10-ear member of the church.

▶ Please join us for our Christmas concert and sin-along.

▶ One of our series of Lenten studies will be a sex-week study of *The Screwtape Letters*.

▶ Newburg Church tries to assist in serving a luncheon for the families of church members who have died immediately following the funeral.

► We invite everyone to our church, no matter what their demonination.

► God provided mammon, a wonderful food to take care of all the nutritional needs of the people.

► The outreach committee has enlisted 25 visitors to make calls on people who are not afflicted with any church.

Gavel to Gabble

DEFENSE ATTORNEY: *If the hand were on the other foot . . .*

"Well, now, Mrs. Bagley," says the lawyer to his client, who has taken the stand. "Tell the court all about it. Do you have a grudge?"

"Oh no," replies Mrs. Bagley. "But we do have a car port."

The lawyer tries again. "Well, does your husband beat you up?"

"No, I'm always the first one out of bed each morning."

"Do you still have relations?"

"Certainly. Two of my aunts, one uncle, and four cousins are still alive."

Growing desperate, the lawyer explains, "What I'm trying to find out is what grounds you have."

"Why, bless you, sir. We live in an apartment, and we don't even have a window box, let alone grounds."

"Mrs. Bagley," shrills the lawyer, now completely out of patience. "What exactly is your reason for seeking a divorce?"

"I'll tell you. It's because my husband and I can't hold an intelligent conversation!"

That swatch of testimony is made up, but exchanges that are just as loopy echo through our halls of justice.

One of the special appeals of courtroom blunders is their unique combination of high drama and low comedy. It is astonishing the regularity with which laughter invades the legal inner sanctum. All lawyers have those days when they think their brains belong to Daniel Webster and Clarence Darrow but their tongues belong to Daffy Duck and Elmer Fudd. Many a witness runs the mouth before engaging the brain and ends up tripping over the tongue while sitting in a stand.

Fortunately, America's army of court reporters are there to snare and then share all the resulting gavel-to-gabble laughter. Here's a full docket of disorder in the court, all on public record, word for word:

> **Q:** Just so I understand: it doesn't hurt when you have sex?
> **A:** No, it doesn't hurt.
> **Q:** Since that time—well, let me put it this way. Nowadays, do you ever have trouble getting an erection?

A: It's harder than before.

Q: What happened next?
A: I woke up unconscious in the hospital.

Q: What is your date of birth?
A: July fifteenth.
Q: What year?
A: Every year.

Q: What gear were you in at the moment of impact?
A: Gucci sweats and Reeboks.

Q: What was the first thing your husband said to you when he woke up that morning?
A: He said, "Where am I, Cathy?"
Q: And why did that upset you?
A: My name is Susan.

Q: Are you sexually active?
A: No, I just lie there.

Defense Attorney: If the hand were on the other foot . . .

Q: Let me get this straight, Mrs. Clarkson. Despite the fact that you had hired detectives to watch your husband's every move, you yourself stood on that corner every night, in all kinds of weather, watching your husband and a woman enter the house, seeing the lights go on downstairs, and then shortly after that in an upstairs bedroom, and then some minutes later turned out entirely. Why in the world did you do it?

A: I just wanted to be near my husband.

A woman charged with adultery was grilled by the opposing attorney:

Q: Young lady, just how do you justify your course of conduct?

A: Well, Judge, I gave him all he wanted. I kept him happy. I don't see why he should be concerned about what I did with my leftovers.

Q: What did you see when the accused took down his pants?

A: Well, it looked like a penis, only smaller.

Q: Well, you're a pretty big man, aren't you?

A: Yes, sir.

Q: How big would you say?

A: Oh, about eight inches.

Q: You don't know what it was, and you don't know what it looked like, but can you describe it?

A: No.

Q: Have you taken any trips out of the state since the accident?

A: Yes.

Q: Where did you go?

A: Georgia.

Q: For what purpose?

A: To funeralize my aunt.

Q: What was your speed at the time of the impact?

A: I don't know how fast I was going because I wasn't looking at the speed thermometer.

Q: How did your accident happen?

A: I was walking across the room and I slipped and fell on a wet spot on my back.

Q: Did the defendant have an erection?

The Defense: Objection. Calls for expert medical opinion.

The Court: I don't think so.

Q: Looking at People's Exhibit 5, a photograph, can you tell me who is in the picture?

A: That's me and Officer Geiger.

Q: Were you there when the picture was taken?

Q: But the anesthesiologist did not assist you in the operation?

A: No.

Q: But merely monitored her unconscious condition and passed gas. That sort of thing, right?

Attorney: Your Honor, I don't want to mislead you down a primrose path.

Q: This myasthenia gravis—does it affect your memory at all?

A: Yes.

Q: And in what ways does it affect your memory?

A: I forget.

Q: You forget. Can you give us an example of something that you've forgotten?

Q: Mr. Smith, I believe your prior testimony before lunch was that you were not arguing with Sam Stevens outside the bar.

A: No.

Q: Is that correct?

A: No, I wasn't.

Q: You were not arguing?

A: No.

Q: No, you were not arguing?

A: No, I wasn't.

Q: You were not arguing.

A: No.

Q: Is it correct that you were not arguing with Mr. Stevens?

A: Yes.
Q: Yes?

Q: How old is your son—the one living with you?
A: Thirty-eight or 35, I can't remember which.
Q: How long has he lived with you?
A: 45 years.

Q: And where was the location of the accident?
A: Approximately milepost 499.
Q: And where is milepost 499?
A: Probably between milepost 498 and 500.

Federal Judge: (from the bench) This seems like a fairly simple problem. Let's not make a federal case out of it.

The Court: Do you have a motion to make at this time?
Attorney: Yes. At this time, Your Honor, we would move that the jury be discharged and the jury be hung because of inability to reach a verdict.

Attorney: (in the middle of a long cross-examination) Your Honor, one of the jurors is asleep.
The Court: Well, you put him to sleep. Now wake him up.

Attorney: And can you show us a copy of that oral agreement?

Q: Sir, what is your IQ?
A: Well, I can see pretty well, I think.

Q: Where did you go next?
A: Over by the hill where all the people conjugate.

Q: Do you have copies of those estimates?
A: I don't know.
Q: Do you have copies of the purchase orders?
A: I don't know.
Q: Do you know who would know?
A: Do I know who would know? Yes.
Q: Who?
A: Me, if I knew.

The Court: Sir, I'm going to have to ask you to answer yes or no because my reporter does not have "uh-huh" and "huh-uh" buttons in her machine. And when you answer "uh-huh" and "huh-uh," she won't have a way to write it. Plus, the jury needs to hear "yes" or "no," not "uh-huh's," and "huh-uh's," okay?
Witness: Uh-huh.

Premedicated Humor

*The patient was bitten by a bat as he walked
down the street on his thumb.*

An Austin, Texas, emergency medical technician answered a call at the home of an elderly woman whose sister had collapsed. As they were placing her into the ambulance, the lady wailed, "Oh, lawdy, lawdy. I know what's the matter with her. She done got the same thing what killed her brother. It's a heretical disease."

The EMT asked what that would be, and the lady said, "The Smiling Mighty Jesus!"

When the EMT got the sister to the county hospital, she looked up the brother's medical records to find he had died of spinal meningitis.

A woman rushed into the lobby of a hospital and exclaimed, "Where's the fraternity ward?" The receptionist calmly replied, "You must mean the maternity ward."

The woman went on, "But I have to see the upturn." Patiently, the receptionist answered, "You must mean the intern."

Exasperated, the woman continued, "Fraternity, maternity, upturn, intern—I don't care wherever or whoever. Even though I use an IOU, and my husband has had a bisectomy, I haven't demonstrated for two months and I think I may be fragrant!"

That same woman later became three centimeters diluted and, narrowly avoiding a mess carriage, she ultimately went into contraptions. Her baby was born with its biblical cord wrapped around its arm, and she asked if she could have the child circumscribed before leaving the hospital.

It is ironic that the humor in hospitals, emergency rooms, and doctors' offices—usually some of the scariest places—can be exceedingly hilarious. The giddy ghost of Mrs. Malaprop haunts medical halls and application forms, where we discover all manner of strange conditions, such as swollen asteroids (adenoids), an erection (anorexia) nervosa, shudders (shingles!), and migrating headaches. All the malappropriate terms in this chapter were miscreated by anxious patients or hassled doctors and nurses.

A man went to his eye doctor, who told him he had a case of myopera and would have to wear contract lenses. That was a lot better than his friend, who had had a cadillac removed from his eye. Still, when he worked at his computer, he would have to watch out for harbor tunnel syndrome. He worried that his authoritis of the joints might be a signal of Old Timer's disease and fretted that

a genital heart defect was causing a myocardial infraction and trouble with his duodemon.

Another man was in the hospital passing gull stones
from his bladder while the doctor was treating a cracked
dish in his spine. After the operation, his glands were
completely prostrated. A hyannis hernia, hanging ham-
meroids, inflammation of the strocum, and a blockage of
his large intesticle could have rendered him impudent.

We're not talking about just a deviant septum here.
These symptoms were enough to give a body heart pop-
ulations, high pretension, a peppery ulcer, and postmor-
tem depression—even a cerebral hemorrhoid. But at least
that's better than a case of headlights (head lice), sea
roses of the liver, cereal palsy, or sick as hell anemia. Any
of these could cause one to slip into a comma.

A woman experienced itching of the virginia during
administration, which led to pulps all up her virginal
area, and they had to void her reproductions. This was
followed by a tubular litigation and, ultimately, mental
pause. Mental pause can cause one to become a maniac
depressive and act like a cyclopath.

She didn't worry about her very close veins, but she
thought that a mammy-o-gram and Pabst smear might
show if she had swollen nymph glands and fireballs of
the eucharist. That's "fibroids of the uterus," and it's
something you can't cure with simple acnepuncture,
Heineken maneuver, or a bare minimum (barium)
enema. Apparently, evasive surgery would be required.
Afterward, she would recuperate in expensive care.

In her introduction to [sic] Humor, a collection of
bloopers from medical transcription, editor Diane S.
Heath writes: "Nobody appreciates a good chuckle more
than the medical transcriptionist who recognizes humor
in the words and situations depicted in daily dictation,

perhaps because it relieves the tension or dispels the gloom associated with the content." Jest for the health of it, here is the lighter side of a profession often preoccupied with tragedy:

► Experienced mood swings because she suffered from PBS.

► The patient is a 32-year-old male who was involved in an altercation with his ex-wife. He suffered a concussion, black eye, and laceration of the arm. She complained of a stress headache from the incident.

► Patient is separated from his wife, and he is also allergic to penicillin.

► The patient was bitten by a bat as he walked down the street on his thumb.

► The young man was seen in my office complaining of involuntary seminal fluids emission during foreplay of several weeks' duration.

► The sound of snoring is due to vibrations of the soft palate and the vulva at the back of the throat.

► On examination here, she was having pain with intercourse.

► The dermatologist made a recommendation for treatment of her face which is not of a serious nature.

► Patient's wife hit him over the head with an ironing board, which now has six stitches in it.

► For his impotence we will discontinue the meds and let his wife handle him.

► She is quite hard of hearing. In fact, she can't hear at all in the left eye.

▶ Her first and only child was born at age 44.

▶ Sinuses run in the family.

▶ She had one fall in April; she attributed this to luck, not circumstance.

▶ He was eating his tray so I didn't examine him.

▶ The patient is a 65-year-old woman who fell, and this fall was complicated by a truck rolling over her.

▶ The patient was lying flat on a guernsey.

▶ Suppositories to be inserted in the rectum at bedtime, after a sitz bath for 12 days.

▶ This 54-year-old female is complaining of abdominal cramps with BMs on the one hand and constipation on the other.

▶ She fell this morning while she was trying to get out of the commode.

▶ The patient was side-swiped by a car riding a motorcycle.

▶ Healthy-appearing, decrepit 69-year-old white female, mentally alert but forgetful.

▶ When she fainted, her eyes rolled around the room.

▶ The patient is a 46-year-old, single, unemployed, retired Hell's Angel.

▶ Further suggested that she avoid using toilet paper and use cotton underwear.

▶ He was advised to force fluids through his interpreter.

▶ He states he hit his head on his forehead.

▶ Her boyfriend also apparently has vaginal warts.

▶ She is to refrain from sexual intercourse until I see her in the office.

▶ The genitalia are normal in experience . . . I'm sorry . . . appearance.

▶ Chief complaint: Auto/pederast accident. History: The patient was a pederast and was struck by an automobile of unknown history.

▶ The patient says he feels so wonderful he wonders what to do with it.

▶ He sleeps on a firm mattress with his legs straight up on his back.

▶ Since the patient stopped smoking, his smell is beginning to return.

▶ The patient is a Catholic nun currently in between missionaries.

▶ He was the first of eight children. His father died at seven.

▶ She has striking red hair and matching brown eyes.

▶ Patient stated that if she would lie down, within two or three minutes something would come across her abdomen and knock her up.

▶ He has an allergy to asthma.

▶ The rest of the physical examination is normal, including the right hands.

▶ Patient has chest pains if she lies on her left side for over a year.

► Patient walks six blocks now. The doctor told him it may take a year to come back.

► The patient and her husband are both trying to get pregnant.

► She has no rigors or shaking chills, but her husband states that she was very hot in bed last night.

Laugh Insurance

EMERGENCY ROOM

"I had to have my armpits removed."
"I was breakdancing, and I think the break broke me."

At the start of World War II, a young man wrote this letter to his draft board:

Dear Sirs:
   This is to notify you of the symptoms I have. Swelling of ankles and feet. Right eye and ear affected by Bell's palsy. Right eye discharges white matter. Both eyes water on contact with wind.
   Left great toe not active because of operation from secondary infraction from bad case of athletic foot. Left great toe develops fever on too much pres-

sure on it, as well as left leg to knee. Left chin bone pains from sunburn two years ago.

Left leg and arm cramps or rheumatism, asthma, and sinus. Believe have touch of TB in lungs—frequent coughing and spitting of matter and substance very gluey and color brownish black. Vomitory in morning. Sometimes blood.

Stomach tender and pains. Burns like fire if drinking orange juice for breakfast. I believe I have ulcers or cancer. Right large intestines have frequent pains. Have had doctor's treatment for it. Piles sometimes bleed.

Continuous colds and head pains, fevers. High or low pressure, probably heart. Spine in my back pains and itches. All teeth ache very bad at times. Perspiration on forehead. Painful bunions on right foot and left bottom foot.

Have inferior complex and nervous conditions, 95% of my acquaintances claim that I am mentally unbalanced. Was kicked in head by a horse when very young.

P.S. I am a patriotic man and I don't want you should think I am trying to get out of draft. If I was, I would exaggerate a little.

People are wondrously creative in describing their aches and pains, and nowhere do we find more creativity than on insurance forms. Claims are normally the most serious part of the insurance business, but humor creeps in every now and then. Here are some explanations for calamitous claims, as received by various insurance company divisions and underwriters. Each is a laugh insurance policy in itself:

► My cartridges are shot.

▶ Fractured 37 ribs.

▶ Fallen buttocks.

▶ The car came at me like a bat out of left field.

▶ An airplane hit the house and came in.

▶ I have athlete's foot on my hands.

▶ I was up a tree after a squirrel, and a guy shot at me.

▶ A broken leg with a severe case of flu.

▶ Hernia from pulling cork out of bottle.

▶ I was crossing the street when a car hit my husband, causing me to break my left foot.

▶ I was making a turn when a car hit me and broke my arm. I no longer own it.

▶ I was looking at weights on bowling balls when a six-pound ball fell on my head.

▶ Getting on a bus, the driver started before I was all in.

▶ While dancing in the navy, someone stepped on my hand.

▶ I fell, hitting my right head.

▶ Accidentally kicked in the stomach by a customary fooling around.

▶ I put tire patch on Playtex girdle and it caused infection in right thigh.

▶ I displaced my shoulder swatting a fly.

▶ I have bad eyes and swell feet.

▶ I suffered burns while holding shirt tail up over an open flame to warm my back.

▶ I keep vomiting on an empty stomach.

▶ I hurt my leg and ever since have been decapitated.

▶ I woke up unconscious.

▶ I am sick now from an absence in my head.

▶ While at work, I was lifting a 60-inch television set and I hurt my back with the help of my co-workers.

▶ While waving good night to a friend, I fell out a two-story window.

▶ Bad corns. Could not wear shoes. Had them removed by surgery.

▶ I broke my foot when I jumped from a 10-foot bank to get down in a ditch so I could get up a tree.

▶ I am an amateur fire-eater. Blowing fire out of mouth, it backfired.

▶ My downfall was a stairway.

▶ I fell from the ceiling at home. Am nervous to work now.

▶ It started with a cough and ended with an appendectomy.

▶ I had the flue with a small touch of ammonia.

▶ Foot broke out and began to run.

▶ My wooden leg was broken when a man hit me with a ranch [wrench].

▶ Headaches and earaches caused by my guitar [goiter].

► Sickness on account of garter [goiter].

► Broken uncle.

► I have romantic fever.

► I had to have my armpits removed.

► I was break-dancing, and I think the break broke me.

► Shortly after the onset of pain, I became pregnant.

► I flunked your analysis test.

Signs of Trouble

On the freight platform of a large station stood a hefty carton on which was printed:

TO AVOID BREAKAGE
KEEP BOTTOM ON TOP

Underneath this, a slightly smaller sign had been pasted:

TOP MARKED BOTTOM
TO AVOID CONFUSION

A sign next to an elevator in the Federal Reserve Bank building in Boston reads:

> IN CASE OF FIRE, EVACUATE THE BUILDING.
> DO NOT USE STAIRWAYS.
> DO NOT USE ELEVATORS.

Above an elevator button in a Denver office building, one finds this sign:

> BRAILLE INSTRUCTIONS
> PLEASE SEE BELOW

We live in the time of the signs, and the examples above cause us to try to find signs of intelligent life on our planet. Here are more signs of the times that tell us it is time to re-sign:

At a tourist spot in Nova Scotia: CAUTION--SLIPPERY ROCKS AND SUDDEN SWELLS AND WAVES RISING ABOVE THE ROCKS EVEN ON FINE AND CALM DAYS HAVE CAUSED MANY ACCIDENTS AND DROWNINGS. ENJOY THEM AT A SAFE DISTANCE.

On bulletin boards at a San Antonio, Texas, hospital: NURSES ARE REQUIRED TO WEAR NOTHING BUT WHITE HOSE.

At the entrance of a college cafeteria: SHOES ARE REQUIRED TO EAT IN THE CAFETERIA. Penciled underneath: SOCKS CAN EAT ANYWHERE THEY WANT.

In a Chicago department store: BARGAIN BASEMENT UP-STAIRS.

At the entrance of Texas A&M–Corpus Christi: NATIONAL COLLEGIATE ALCOHOL AWARENESS WEEK—FREE DRINKS IN STU-DENT CENTER LOUNGE.

In front of a Canton, Massachusetts, filling station: OUR REST ROOMS ARE CLEAN AROUND THE CLOCK. (What about the rest of the room?)

Near a London hospital:

HOSPITAL
PLEASE GO QUIETLY

Near Heathrow Airport: TWA--FLIGHTS TO THE UNITED STATES AND CALIFORNIA.

In the window of a Boston supermarket: FOR YOUR SHOPPING CONVENIENCE WE WILL BE CLOSED CHRISTMAS DAY, DEC. 25.

In a Santa Fe, New Mexico, open-air market:

FLEA MARKET
NO DOGS

Two signs, one over the other, in Seattle: PLANNED PARENTHOOD/FREE DELIVERY.

On a traffic light in Newport, New Hampshire: OFFICER AHEAD/WHEN FLASHING.

On a Newark, New Jersey, government office building: THE STATE OF NEW JERSEY HAS MOVED FOUR BLOCKS WEST.

In the window of a Woodsville, Washington, store:

OUT OF BUSINESS
THANKS TO OUR CUSTOMERS

On the door of a men's room in West Virginia:

MEN
SLIPPERY
WHEN
WET

Over cash register in a Seattle clothing store: WE DON'T CHANGE UNDERWEAR.

In a San Diego laundromat: NO TINTING OR DYING IN MACHINE.

On a Jacksonville, North Carolina, street:

ABSOLUTELY
NO
PARKING
ENFORCED

On a Hendersonville, North Carolina, restaurant: OPEN. GREAT FOOD 'TIL 11 P.M.

In the produce section of a Kitty Hawk, North Carolina, market: IF THE PACKAGE SIZE YOU WANT IS NOT ON DISPLAY, PLEASE SEE THE PERISHABLE MANAGER.

Painted on the side of a pickup truck:

SAUSAGE DELI
TUCSON'S ALTERNATIVE TO FINE DINING

On a Minneapolis motel: MARIA'S BREAKFAST CLUB: NOW OPEN EVENINGS.

Outside a Tampa restaurant:

FRIED CLAMS
PARK HERE

At the approach to a bridge in New London, Connecticut: STOP ON WHITE LINE WHEN RED.

In a fast-food eatery: IF YOUR ORDER IS NOT SATISFACTORY, PLEASE RETURN THE PRODUCT TO THE COUNTER AND WE WILL REPLACE IT WITH A SMILE.

Outside a cabinetmaker's shop in Sperryville, Virginia:

ANTIQUE TABLES
MADE DAILY

In front of a Parkville, Maryland, seafood store: PARKING FOR PARKVILLE CRABS ONLY.

On a Newton, Massachusetts, club:

LIVE LOBSTERS
DANCING NIGHTLY

Sign outside a barbecue restaurant in Atlanta: NOW ACCEPT-
ING APPLICATIONS FOR COOKS BETWEEN 2 AND 5.

In a pet shop: LARGE BIRDS REDUCED.

In a Naples, New York, cemetery: POSITIVELY NO HOLES DUG
IN THIS CEMETERY.

At a Sandwich, Massachusetts, diner: WE GUARANTEE FAST
SERVICE NO MATTER HOW LONG IT TAKES.

In the bathroom of a Chinese restaurant in Detroit: EMPLOY-
EES MUST WASH YOUR HANDS.

On a farm near Elizabethtown, Kentucky: USED COWS FOR
SALE.

In auto-repair garage in Seattle: WE ARE SORRY BUT WE CAN-
NOT ACCEPT ANY CUSTOMER PARTS OR FLUIDS.

At some Kentucky Fried Chicken restaurants: PARKING FOR
KENTUCKY FRIED CUSTOMERS ONLY.

At a truck stop in Tulsa, Oklahoma: KIDS WITH GAS EAT
FREE.

In the Glasgow, Scotland, airport: HUMPED PEDESTRIAN
CROSSING.

By the road near Cape May, New Jersey:

BLUEPOINT OYSTERS
OPENED
WHILE YOU WAIT
IN THEIR OWN JUICE

On a back road in Washington State:

NEW AND USED ANTIQUES
COME IN
WE ARE CLOSED

In a Bridgewater, New Jersey, bookstore, advertising a cook-book writer: AUTHOR SIGNING AND TASTING.

In the Mammoth Caves in Virginia: BOTTOMLESS PIT—175 FEET DEEP.

At the entrance of a one-way bridge in Sonoma, California: WHEN THIS SIGN IS UNDERWATER, THIS ROAD IS IMPASSABLE.

In a Kalamazoo, Michigan, department store:

WE HAVE BUTTON-FLY LEVIS
OPEN TILL 10 TONITE.

At a diet center in Poughkeepsie, New York: LOSE ALL YOUR WEIGHT: $198.

In a Los Angeles dance studio: DUE TO CIRCUMSTANCES BE-YOND OUR CONTROL DANCE LESSONS WILL RESUME NEXT WEEK.

At the entrance to a bridge in Philadelphia:

IN CASE OF ENEMY ATTACK
DO NOT STOP
DRIVE RIGHT OFF BRIDGE

In a Portland, Maine, parking garage: TENANTS NOT PAID BY THE 15TH OF THE MONTH WILL BE TERMINATED.

In a Brooklyn barbershop window: DURING CONSTRUCTION WE WILL SHAVE YOU IN THE REAR.

In a Baltimore restaurant: ALL FOOD MUST PASS THROUGH THE CASHIER BEFORE ENTERING THE DINING ROOM.

III

COLD OFF
THE PRESS

Headline Headaches

*INCLUDE YOUR CHILDREN
WHEN BAKING COOKIES.*

In late summer, *The Dallas Morning News* published a special back-to-school section that covered new trends in education and new personnel, curriculum, and physical changes in the Dallas school system. Such a special section is often called an "extra," so the bright-red headline that lit up the top of the *Morning News* front page was:

TEXAS COLLEGES STILL A BARGAIN, EDUCATION EXTRA

Readers may have thought that Texas colleges were a good deal—as long as you weren't seeking to learn anything. Hey, we've got great cheerleaders, but we charge extra for courses in calculus.

Sometimes you need to know the context of a headline in order to guess what it's trying to announce:

MONTANA TRADED TO KANSAS CITY

Explanation: San Francisco 49ers quarterback Joe Montana was traded to the Kansas City Chiefs.

DEAD GUITARIST NOW SLIMMER AND TRIMMER

Explanation: Grateful Dead guitarist Jerry Garcia was on a diet.

HARRIS AHEAD BUT DANG LIKELY TO FORCE RUNOFF

Explanation: Oakland, California, Mayor Elihu Harris faced an election runoff against businessman Ted Dang.

SENTINEL NAMES SOBER FEMALE ATHLETE OF YEAR

Explanation: An athlete named Erin Sober was being honored.

LITTLE PEOPLE STRIKE VICTIMS

Explanation: It's the people with small businesses, not the players, who suffered most from the 1994 baseball strike.

JUST HOW LONG DOES IT TAKE
FACIAL HAIR TO GROW A FOOT?

Explanation: A man can figure he'll add another inch to his beard every eight weeks.

Now we can turn to the "How's That Again?" Department. Some call these examples blinkers because, quite simply, they make the reader blink:

FRIED CHICKEN COOKED
IN MICROWAVE WINS TRIP

AFTER DETOUR TO CALIFORNIA
SHUTTLE RETURNS TO EARTH

MAN JUMPS OFF 2ND STREET BRIDGE
NEITHER JUMPER NOR BODY FOUND

LEGISLATOR WANTS TOUGHER DEATH PENALTY

INCLUDE YOUR CHILDREN WHEN BAKING COOKIES

LEARNING TO SKI AN UPHILL BATTLE, EXPERTS SAY

WOMAN IMPROVING AFTER FATAL CRASH

MANY WHO MOVE TO FLORIDA
LEAVE AFTER DEATH

PROPERLY DRAFTED WILL
REDUCES ANXIETY AFTER DEATH

FLIER TO DUPLICATE
MISS EARHART'S FATAL FLIGHT

BOY DECLARED DEAD, REVIVES
AS FAMILY PROTESTS

MOTHER OF 18 CHILDREN IN TROUBLE AGAIN

SUICIDE BOMBERS STRIKE AGAIN

DEAD COYOTE FOUND IN BRONX
LAUNCHES SEARCH FOR ITS MATE

STUDY: THOSE WITHOUT
INSURANCE DIE MORE OFTEN

42 PERCENT OF ALL MURDERED WOMEN
ARE KILLED BY THE SAME MAN

EXPERTS INCREASE PROBABILITY
OF BIG QUAKE IN CALIFORNIA

PREVENT INJURIES TO BABY
MICROWAVE SAFELY

WOMAN FATALLY MAULED
ASSIGNED INDOOR JOB

Close kin to the blinker is the penetrating glimpse into the obvious. These self-evident headlines make us say, "Quite so. What's the big deal?"

JAIL MAY HAVE TO CLOSE DOORS

MAN FOUND DEAD IN CEMETERY

GUNFIRE IN SARAJEVO THREATENS CEASEFIRE

ACTOR'S DEATH DURING FILMING
USUALLY CAREER-LIMITING MOVE

RELIGION PLAYS MAJOR PART
IN MESSAGE OF EASTER

CITY HALL SAYS FLOODING IN LOWLANDS
WAS THE RESULT OF TOO MUCH WATER

DROWNING OFTEN CAUSE OF DEATH IN OKLAHOMA

STUDY: DEAD PATIENTS USUALLY NOT SAVED

EXTINCT ANIMALS MAY LOSE PROTECTION

STUDENTS AT COLLEGES GROW OLDER

WARRING FACTIONS DON'T AGREE

CHILDBIRTH IS BIG STEP TO PARENTHOOD

MEMORIZATION ABILITY
ATTRIBUTED TO BRAIN USE

LOW WAGES SAID KEY TO POVERTY

STUDY FINDS SEX, PREGNANCY LINK

ONLY RAIN WILL CURE DROUGHT

ECONOMIST USES THEORY TO EXPLAIN ECONOMY

BIBLE CHURCH'S FOCUS IS THE BIBLE

WHATEVER THEIR MOTIVES,
MOMS WHO KILL KIDS STILL SHOCK US

ALCOHOL ADS PROMOTE DRINKING

FREE ADVICE: BUNDLE UP WHEN OUT IN COLD

Banner Boners

SHOP SELLS SOUP TO NUTS

Headlines are literally the head lines, the most prominent part of a newspaper. Thus, when a headline runs amock and becomes a mockery, the error is there for all to see. It has been said that the pun is the lowest form of wit. When an editor inadvertently trips over a double meaning, the result can be the lowest form of headline:

NATIONAL HUNTING GROUP TARGETING WOMEN

HIGH COURT TO HEAR MARIJUANA CASE

TEEN ATTEMPTS TO QUIT SMOKING COLD TURKEY

LEGISLATORS TAX BRAINS TO CUT DEFICIT

CELEBRITIES RUB SHOULDERS ON SLOPES

PARTIAL JURY CHOSEN FOR TYSON CASE

SCHOOL TAXPAYERS REVOLTING

"WOMEN IN POLITICS" WORKSHOP
POSTPONED; MAKE-UP NOT SET

STARVING ANGOLANS EATING DOGS, BARK

PRINCE CHARLES BACKS BICYCLES
OVER CARS AS HE OPENS WORLD TALKS

CRACK FOUND IN AUSTRALIA

IOWA MAN'S SOON-TO-BE AMPUTATED
HAND COULD HOLD KEY TO MURDER

ARMLESS MUSICIAN TOUCHES AUDIENCE

ONE-LEGGED ESCAPEE STILL ON RUN

MAN MINUS EAR WAIVES HEARING

CELLULAR PHONES GROWING ON FARM

BEACHES ALL WASHED UP

ADMIRAL LIKES TO MAKE WAVES

MAN, 68, GETS 5 YEARS IN CRACK VIAL CASE

FIRST BLACK MAYOR, 5 RACES STILL UNDECIDED

BAR TRYING TO HELP ALCOHOLIC LAWYERS

NY MAYORAL CANDIDATES
DEBATE CRIME FIGURES

DON'T TIE MY HANDS ON ARMS,
REAGAN ASKS RADIO AUDIENCE

CRASH VICTIM LEAVES
A HOLE IN HER COMMUNITY

BOND ISSUE IS HELD OVER CITY INCINERATOR

SHOP SELLS SOUP TO NUTS

BUXOM STARLET KNOCKED FLAT BY FANS

FIRE OFFICIALS GRILLED
OVER KEROSENE HEATERS

POLICE SEEK AID FROM PUBLIC
IN SLAYING OF MAN

Sometimes the accidental pun turns on a quirk of grammar. Many headlines turn out to be grammatical minefields. Especially within the tight boundaries of a few picas, grammatical bombs can explode in an editor's face:

CLINTON VISITS HURT SOLDIERS

PREVENTIVE HEALTH SERVICE
FOR WOMEN BEING CUT IN HALF

TWO CARS COLLIDE,
ONE SENT TO HOSPITAL

SMITHSONIAN MAY CANCEL
BOMBING OF JAPAN EXHIBIT

U.S. SHIPS HEAD TO SOMALIA

HIGH SCHOOL HONORS STUDENTS
ARRESTED FOR HATE CRIMES

DOCTORS HELP TORCH VICTIM

VOTER FEARS ALERT POLITICIANS

FBI AGENT IN SUBWAY
SHOOTS MAN WITH KNIFE

2 SHIPS COLLIDE IN MANILA BAY;
FERRY CARRYING 500 SINKS

10% OF STUDENTS FAIL CLASSES FOR TRUANCY

YOUTH HIT BY CAR RIDING BICYCLE

FONDA GIVES POOR
EXERCISE, ACTING TIPS

ASTRONAUTS PRACTICE
LANDING ON LAPTOPS

POLICE CAN'T STOP GAMBLING

POLICE NAB STUDENTS WITH PAIR OF PLIERS

$1 MILLION GIVEN TO BETTER SLUMS

HOW TO COMBAT THAT FEELING
OF HELPLESSNESS WITH ILLEGAL DRUGS

Galley Oops!

Smoke bellowed from the windows.

The late Denys Parsons, British master collector of newspaper and magazine bloopers, created a specter named Gobfrey Shrdlu. Parsons decribed Shrdlu as "a malicious spirit with an irresistible sense of humour who lurks at the elbow of tired reporters, editors, and printers, with disastrous consequences."

My research indicates that Shrdlu was born during the reign of Charles I, when a court printer produced a handsome edition of the Bible. In it, some overworked typesetter or editor omitted the little word *not* from the seventh commandment so that it read: "Thou shalt commit adultery." As a result, that edition became known as The Adulterous Bible.

"Thou shalt commit adultery" was one of the very first printed bloopers, and the tradition of falling pratfully in public print has continued undimmed. Surely the irrepressible Shrdlu had a wispy hand in the creation of the following all-American galley gaffes:

► This afternoon, firemen battled a skyscraper fire in New York. It was confined to the upper floor, where smoke bellowed from the windows.

► The crime bill passed by the Senate would reinstate the federal death penalty for certain violent crimes: assassinating the president, hijacking an airline, and murdering a government poultry inspector.

► He came back to Sanford during the Depression to practice law with his father, Hiram, whose brother and law partner had just died and who needed help.

► The ordinance approved Tuesday night would impose a moratorium on all breeding by dog and cat owners for six months beginning in July.

► Political insiders call them wedge issues—raw, emotional issues like social security for Democrats and capital punishment for Republicans.

► The race also includes two of the five openly gay candidates running around the city.

► The pro–seat belt camp maintains that seat belts would keep students, particularly smaller children like Marvin, from being thrown from their seats and escaping serious injury.

► The department has implemented a computerized system for tracking down dead beat parents.

► Vincent Charles, a 14-year Secret Service veteran, said the string of incidents had heightened security around the White House. "The White House has always attracted the mentally ill," he said.

► Coach Mike Kyzyzewski asked some of his players over to the house for dinner one day last spring, then barbecued himself.

► "One in 20 women will be stalking victims at some time in their lives," said Rep. Carlin Cody, R-Hatfield, Texas.

► This is the third marriage of the groom. He has also been through World War II.

► After a Rastafarian had run amok and amputated one of his mother's and both of his father's hands, a police source described their conditions as serious. "They will just have to keep their fingers crossed," he said.

► Why would a young mother wait nine hours in line to get front-row tickets to a show? The Mighty Morphine Power Rangers, friends.

► The dead man was described as white, aged between 30 and 40, with an Irish accent.

► From now on, police will pick up road-killed animals, not Public Works employees.

► *I Spy* returns. Secret agents (Robert Culp, Bill Cosby) from the 1960s TV series reunite on a case, joined by their son and daughter.

► Spike Lee says his new movie *Malcolm X* ends in the townships of South Africa, not the Harlem ballroom where the black nationalist leader was assassinated for artistic reasons.

▶ Smith was one of 10 Dallas businessmen robbed and brutally beaten with aluminum baseball bats from October to January.

▶ How we feel about ourselves is the core of self-esteem, says author Mary Anne Hunter.

▶ Q. Why don't women's blouses come in sleeve lengths, like men's shirts?

A. Because there is no standard sleeve length for women's blouses. Men's long-sleeve shirts are designed to be worn with a jacket so that the sleeve will hang just below the wrist line when the wearer is standing. But women wear long-sleeve blouses with other garments or no covering at all.

▶ During the scrimmage, [Fresno State University basketball coach Jerry] Tarkanian paced the sideline with his hands in his pockets while biting his nails.

▶ Garden club members heard a talk on bugs and roaches. A large number were present.

▶ In women twice as often as in men, death was the first sign that HIV was progressing, the researchers found.

▶ The fiftieth anniversary of the bombing of Dresden by the Royal Air Force and the U.S. Army Air Forces is being observed today in Britain as an act of retaliation for the bombing of Coventry by the Luftwäffe on Nov. 14, 1940.

▶ HELP WITH KIDS. Colorado families with more than 5,000 children have sought help finding child care from the new, free Colorado Office of Resource and Referral Agencies.

▶ Jazz tunes, including "Modern Leaves," "Scrapple

from the Apple," and "The Girl with Emphysema," stopped at 8:30, when the volunteer trip packed up.

▶ An American teenager gives birth every 20 minutes.

▶ Seven pages of the biography are devoted to revelations about Coco Chanel's habit of cooling champagne by pouring it over a block of ice, her rock crystal collection, her brown pillows, and her paneled closets.

▶ Japanese tabloids are all atwitter that the wife of Crown Prince Naruhito, whose years-long search for a bride was exhaustively chronicled, might soon be a father.

▶ NOTICE: I wish to thank anyone who so kindly assisted in my husband's death.

▶ Arthritis support groups: For family and friends and all types of arthritis, including lupus and fibromyalgia.

▶ There are no national temperatures today due to transmission difficulties.

▶ The Southeast Georgia Alzheimer's Chapter will present a cabaret, "A Night to Remember."

▶ If you ask the average American for a detailed description of the bed he sleeps in, he will probably be unable to oblige you. He can precisely visualize his overcoats, his golf clubs, or his automobile, but his bed and furniture in general are merely nebulous conveniences in his mind. And the same thing is true of his wife.

All the Nudes Fit to Print

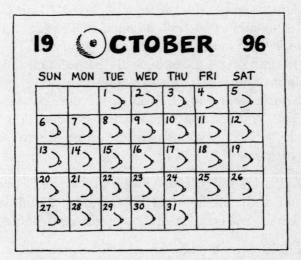

OCTOBER IS BREAST AWARENESS MONTH.

Possibly the most embarrassing modern-day typographical error—due to the slip of an unknown typo writer—appeared in *The Washington Post* in 1915. In a news story, it was noted that President Woodrow Wilson had taken his fiancée Edith Galt to the theater the previous night and, rather than watching the play, "spent most of his time entering Mrs. Galt." The writer meant "entertaining."

Another story included a photograph of a famous president and popular funny man. The below-par caption read: "President Richard Nixon watches comedian

Jackie Gleason tee off on the first hole as they started a golf match in Miami Sunday. The president's first shot went high and off to the left about 100 yards. But he didn't look bad compared with Gleason, who sliced his first shot to the right and teed off again, sending a grass-cutter fart to the left."

More recently, a news story reported, "Ivan Gorlen drove his motorcycle into a lamppost 12 years ago and in an instant severed not only the cartilage in his knee but his grip on the gleaming balls that were his life."

Turns out that Gorlen was a bowler.

"Sextra! Sextra! Read all about it!" newspapers seem to blare. It's amazing how lewd, lascivious, licentious, and lecherous are so many of the errors in newspapers and magazines:

▶ Katherine Innes, as the virgin in this year's production of the Passion Play, has already started her rehearsal. She is the first blond virgin for a century.

▶ The Oregon Republican admits he harassed women but vows not to quit.

▶ Matson, of Phelps County, is recuperating from wounds inflicted two weeks ago when an unknown assailant fired a shotgun at his backside. About 800 marijuana plants have been discovered in the same area.

▶ Barton, it is claimed, was driving at a high rate of speed and swerving from side to side. As he approached the crossing, he started directly towards it and crashed into Miss Palmer's rear end, which was sticking out into the road about a foot. Luckily she escaped injury and the damage can easily be remedied with a new coat of paint.

▶ Jerry Lee Lewis played the piano with his elbow, feet, and any other part of his body available.

▶ The Misses Doris, Agnes, and Vivian Jameson are spending several days at the home of their mother. This is the first time in years that the community has had the pleasure of seeing the Jameson girls in the altogether.

▶ Bronstein, a UNH entymologist, is an expert on insects that bite people in recreation areas.

▶ Policeman Bart Grayson was shot through the stomach and Bill Maybury, Indiana Harbor taxi driver, through the hip, while a guard at the jail was shot in the excitement.

▶ The bits about masturbation are especially well handled.

▶ In a wanton display of chastity, more than 100,000 Southern Baptist youngsters are pledging to abstain from sex until marriage.

It is in the art of headline writing that journalists show themselves to be so wanton that they sometimes land in the soup. *The Washington Post* printed this headline on the front page of its first edition: FDR IN BED WITH COED. Actually President Roosevelt was in bed with a cold, as the story made clear.

The New Orleans *Morning Tribune* ran a story covering King Edward's courtship of Mrs. Wallace Simpson. The headline: GIVES KING TWO DAYS ON WALLY.

Many a suggestive headline is explained with a little background information:

MANLY MAN MARRIES FERTILE WOMAN
Explanation: A man from Manly, Minnesota, married a woman from Fertile, in the same state.

LAY TEACHERS FOR FIRST TIME IN SCHOOLS

Explanation: A local Catholic school can no longer fill its staff with nuns.

CHICK ACCUSES SOME OF HER
MALE COLLEAGUES OF SEXISM

Explanation: Los Angeles councilwoman Laura Chick lashed out at City Hall as the "most sexist good-old-boys environment that I've ever been in."

IDAHO BRIDES CAN'T TAKE HEAVY G.I. TRAFFIC

Explanation: The story is about Idaho *bridges*, but the printer carelessly dropped a *g*.

VIRGIN TO PROVIDE WEEKEND EXCITEMENT

Explanation: Famous runner Craig Virgin will enter the local race.

SURGERY FOR BUTTS

Explanation: New England Patriots running back Marion Butts needs an operation.

HELEN WILLS MOODY ON 3-WEEK HONEYMOON

Explanation: Tennis champion Helen Wills Moody is on her honeymoon.

BRANDEIS PLAYERS MASTER BATES

Explanation: Brandeis University defeated Bates College in football.

RECORD SOVIET CROP: TURD

Explanation: Crop production was announced by the communist news outlet Trud—creating an accident waiting to happen.

ALLIES PUSH BOTTLES UP 10,000 GERMANS
Translation: Advances by the Allied forces in World
War II contained the German forces.

Here are some more headlines that would keep Sig-
mund Freud busy for many sessions:

FREE VACCINATIONS SOUGHT
FOR EVERY CHILD BY CLINTON

SEMINAL ISSUE RESURFACES
IN PRISONERS' SUITS

PRIVATES HELD IN SEXUAL ASSAULT

ADULTS THINK TEENS HAVING
MORE SEX THAN THEY ARE

AWALT READY TO PLUG
BILL'S HOLE AT TIGHT END

LAY POSITION PROPOSED
BY BISHOP FOR WOMEN

BARBARA BUSH TALKS ABOUT HER LIFE,
ABORTION, HOMOSEXUALITY

TEEN SEX DELAYED WHEN DAD'S AROUND

FUMES FORCE HUGE NOGALES EVACUATION

WIFE LOSES 86 POUNDS BEFORE HUSBAND COMES

PECK RECALLS MOBY DICK AS HIS HARDEST

OCTOBER IS BREAST AWARENESS MONTH

BOY WANTS TO MOUNT AUTOGRAPHED GUITAR

AFTER SPILL, JOCKEY'S BUSINESS FALLS OFF

FRENCH DAM SITE BETTER OFF WITH U.S. AID FUNDS

ADMIRALS AXED FOR ROLL IN TAILHOOK

BRISBANE BROKEN DOWN BY AGE AND SEX

POWER POLE ERECTION CUTS
POWER IN CHALAN PAGO

POLICE WANT TO SEE MORE
OF MAN WHO EXPOSED SELF

MARY SMITH TO PRESENT RECTAL

PROBE UNDERWAY ON STRIPPER

EX-FIREMAN STARTS PRISON FOR SEX CRIMES

TAXIS TRY FLASHERS

We Stand Korrected

Mr. Hoffnagle is, of course, a detective on the police farce.

"Our paper carried the notice last week that Mr. Oscar Hoffnagle is a defective on the police force. This was a typographical error. Mr. Hoffnagle is, of course, a detective on the police farce."

It has been said that journalism is the first rough draft of history. Reporting can also be the first rough draft of more accurate reporting in the form of "corrections" that appear a day or two after the original stories. The problem is that sometimes corrections turn out to be defectives on the paper's policing farce. At other times, the corrections that turn out to be incorrections make you wonder what the newspaper is trying to correct:

▶ The marriage of Miss Frieda van Amburg and Willie Branton, which was announced in this paper a few weeks ago, was a mistake which we wish to correct.

▶ A news analysis article on Saturday about the politics behind Gov. Pete Wilson's role in eliminating affirmative-action programs at University of California campuses rendered a word incorrectly in a question from Sherry Bebitch Jeffe, a former legislative aide in Sacramento.

   Ms. Jeffe said of Mr. Wilson: "He's biding his time on this, knowing all along what he was going to do when the time was ripe. It's ripe. He's picked." She did not say, "He's pickled."

▶ An interview with Mary Matalin, the former deputy manager of the Bush campaign, quoted her incorrectly on the talk show host Rush Limbaugh. She said he was "sui generis," not "sweet, generous."

▶ The Pacific Rim column in yesterday's Business/ Extra section should have read that "*Fine Boys* is a leading Japanese fashion magazine for guys," not gays. The *Chronicle* regrets the editing error.

▶ Rape suspect Fred A. Zaroff told state police September 16 that he had sex with a 25-year-old woman, but it was "not a rape," according to testimony in the Crown County Court. A story in Monday's *Times* incorrectly said that Zaroff told troopers sex with the woman was "not that great."

▶ Because of a telephone transcription error, an article yesterday about Mary Allison Graves, a lawyer, included an erroneous description. The first sentence should have begun, "Attorney Mary Allison Graves," not "A tiny Mary Allison graves." Ms. Graves is 5 foot 7.

► An item in our newspaper erred in reporting that a cash bar will be part of the First United Church's Back-to-School Bash on Friday. A "car bash" will be part of the event.

► Our report on Monday said that up to 6 million had died in a gun battle in Sri Lanka. It should have read up to 6 militants died in a gun battle.

► We would like to point out that the previous writer on the subject, who was referred to as Miss Turner, was in fact Ms. Turner, not Mrs. Davis as we stated last week.

► Due to an error, the October 22 story on the ABC bond read that John Gorham said "diddly squat" when asked to explain consultant recommendations in the bond. The story should have read that we were unable to reach Gorham for comment. We apologize for the error.

► The article about the Ladies' Craft Club should have stated that Mrs. Brown and Mrs. Smith have talks on "smocking and rugs," not "smoking and drugs," as previously reported.

► There was a typo in lawyer Griswold's ad. His logo name is: "Your case is no stronger than your attorney," not "stranger."

► For the old-style corn chowder recipe from the Wooden Spoon column: Add one big onion, not one bag of onions.

► An article in Saturday's local edition incorrectly reported that a suspect who had been indicted by a federal grand jury had been identified as "Fnu Lnu." "Fnu Lnu" is not a name. "Fnu" is a law-enforcement abbreviation for "first name unknown," "Lnu" for "last name unknown."

► Burlington County Commissioner Bert Greenough has 100 percent support from his family, not 10 percent, as was stated in last week's article on Greenough's announcement to seek re-election.

► The "Candidates on Television" listing yesterday misspelled the name of the vice president in some editions. It is Quayle, not Quale. The *Tmise* regrets the error.

► The Auctions column in Weekend yesterday misidentified a brand of watch. It is a World Time, not a Waldheim. [Oh well, that's what happens when you forget to Adenhauer.]

And especially loopy is this incorrection:

► Erroneous information was inadvertently inserted into the biographical summary accompanying a story on Joseph Argyle. Mr. Argyle cannot simultaneously whistle, stand on his head, and drink beer.

Classified Classics

Conscious Attorney

A company ran an advertisement for a portable camp shower, emphasizing the ease with which it could be assembled. In a full-page ad, showing a bikini-clad woman screwing the shower to the wall, the big, black headline read: TWO SCREWS AND YOU'RE READY FOR A SHOWER.

Encyclopaedia Brittanica's boxed ad in the Yellow Pages prominently featured the following slogan in both boldface and quotation marks: **"Crib Through College."**

A Manitoba reader winged me this advertisement for a Kentucky Fried Chicken "event:"

KFC Express!
Grand Opening Special
"Super Value Meal Deal"
10 pieces of children, 5 hot wings,
large taters, large salad,
and one liter ice cream for only $19.99.

"It makes you wonder what KFC stands for, doesn't it?" quipped the reader.

Sure does, and it makes you wonder if anybody is out there proofreading all those advertisements that bombard us every day in an ad, ad, ad, ad world. As a seniors center's flier advises, "Please Patronize Our Advertisers." The following ads deserve our most fervent patronization:

► Giant Stuff-A-Pumpkin Bag. Have fun stuffing this giant pumpkin with friends & family. Great Halloween parties!

► Beautiful rocking baby cradle, solid cherry, 110 years old, original owner.

► Use our medicine and you can kiss your hemorrhoids goodbye!

► Kinney shoe stores: We only sell the right shoe.

► Our goal is to have you drive away a satisfied customer.

► Van—'94 Dodge Grand Caravan. One owner, lady driver, loaded.

► Feline Ultramilk is a low-lactose milk replacement for cats packaged in a disposable carton.

► The Best Collection of Enticing Lingerie! The dazzling

lingerie that California women are wearing is now available to you.

▶ Listing in Tucson, Arizona, Yellow Pages: Antidefecation League of B'Nai B'Rith.

▶ Turkey Carpet for Sale good condition the property of a lady too large for her rooms.

▶ In a flier for a child-abuse charity golf tournament: To stop child abuse, shoot a hole in one.

▶ ATTENTION CUSTOMERS. Due to flooding at a Proctor & Gamble plant in Albany, Georgia, we are experiencing some temporary out of stocks on Bounty Towels.

▶ On Red Cross cards asking recipients to donate their blood: Give blood again. It will be felt for a lifetime.

▶ MEDICAL MALPRACTICE. Former military attorneys specializing in claims arising out of military and VA hospitals. Free Consultation—No Fee Unless You Recover.

▶ Narcolepsy Support Group, a new group for individuals who suffer from this sleep disorder and their families, will begin at 2 P.M.

▶ Man with power, two sweet to be sour. Successful real estate typhoon, 40, 6'3", handsome, muscular, gentle, fun-loving, adventurous.

▶ Law-firm ad: If you have experienced accident, injury, or even death, please call us.

▶ Conscious Attorney. 11 years' experience. Brooklyn, Manhattan locations.

▶ In a brochure advertising a seminar on sexual harassment in the workplace: Experts will define issues, clarify laws, and conduct hands-on training.

▶ *On a menu in Healdsburg, California:* Two fried eggs, any style.

▶ Bras—$^1/_2$ Off!

▶ WANTED. Looking for hanging cage for my daughter. Must have exercise wheel.

▶ WANTED. Help for parents of children with attention deficit and lystexia.

▶ WANTED. 100-year-old bridge repairers.

▶ WANTED. A steady young woman to wash, iron, and milk two cows.

▶ WANTED. Boring Mill Operator.

▶ WANTED. Waitresses. Male or female may apply.

▶ WANTED. Emotionally Handicapped Teacher.

▶ WANTED. A boy to open oysters 15 years old.

▶ FOR SALE. Pointsetters, from 4 inches to 4 feet high.

▶ FOR SALE. Stimulated pearls.

▶ All Satin Shoes $9.99. Dying $4.99 extra.

▶ XYZ Motors is the oldest Saab dealer in the Upper Valley since 1968.

▶ Sensual Aides: How to order them without embarrassment. How to use them without disappointment.

▶ Osculating fan. Great Value. Only $8.93.

▶ Cupid's Restaurant. Beautiful ladies to serve you. We've Upped Our Standards. Up Yours.

▶ Equestrian Mom seeks pony or horse to rent to teach English to kids 5 & 7.

► There will be plenty to eat: hot dogs, hamburgers, children under 12, only a dollar.

► Laser Surgery Available for the Prostrate.

► Waterproof pigskin suede protects your ankles and feet in cool and incontinent weather.

► Widow, 73, would like to meet gent with a car of similar age.

► Consummate your marriage in one of our beautiful gowns.

► New and used hay and firewood for sale.

► Sale: Tires Slashed!

► Epoxy Rock, a durable, high-quality surface, is guaranteed for life. Never resurface again with Epoxy Rock.

► At the Cleveland Clinic, some of our surgeons can add years to your life. Others are equally expert at reversing the process.

► Mattie's. Yogurt and Ice Cream Parlor
   "An Alternative to Good Eating"

► Wow! Ferrari, red, with buckskin leather: 1984 308 GTSi QV, 1 owner with removable top.

► Treadmill $100, stair-stepper $75, mini trampoline $10, Thigh master $10, crutches $10.

► Dentistry for Adults and Children: Emergency Services Available, Quality Dentistry for All Ages, Strict Sterilization Between Patients.

► Grand piano for sale by young lady with mahogany legs.

▶ Our Brake and Tire Service Will Keep You Coming Back.

▶ Mattress company slogan: Why Not Sleep With the Best?

▶ Men and Women Heels: $1/2$ Price.

▶ Apple Brown Betty—$4.00. Heated with vanilla ice cream.

▶ Picked Fence, white 4×8, $7

▶ GLASS. 24 hours. Day or night.

▶ Special This Week in the Service Dept. at Jim Jakes Chevrolet: Front Brake Job, Inspect Rears.

▶ ATTENTION: If you're looking for a quiet lot with a large pond for your mobile home, we have the place for you.

▶ Will swap new handmade pairs of shorts for your child, sizes 2–6, for a weekend stay at your bed-and-breakfast.

▶ On a Mexican take-out menu: Melted Cheese on a flour tortilla, topped with chili, sour cream, and glaucoma.

▶ On a grocery bag: Save-Rite Proudly Supports Muscular Dystrophy.

▶ Allow me to recycle your unwanted children and infant clothing. Free pickup.

▶ Ace termite and pest control. Complete satisfaction or your money back. Ideal for children and pets.

▶ Sale: All Furniture Slashed!

Finally, this most classic of classified gems:

LOST DOG—Mixed breed, shaggy, left front leg amputated, missing top of right ear, partially blind, bad case of mange, tail was broken and healed crooked, some teeth gone, scars on head and back, has been castrated. Answers to name of Lucky.

IV

CLEAR AS MUDDLE

Fractured English Abroad

Go soothingly on the grease mind as there lurk the skid demon.

In 1962, during the Cuban missile crisis, Secretary of State Dean Rusk announced, "We're eyeball to eyeball and I think the other fellow just blinked." Soviet Foreign Minister Andrei Gromyko responded to the comment by announcing, "I am looking forward to talking with you balls to balls."

When a French-Canadian politician was applauded by an American audience, he beamed, saying, "I thank you for giving my wife and me the clap! I thank you from the heart of my bottom and my wife thanks you from her bottom too!"

These charming efforts remind us that few idioms and expressions can be literally translated word for word from one language to another. Every traveler and tourist in a foreign land has a tale to tell about the fractured English of signs, menus, and advertisements.

A classic of global gabble is this list of Japanese rules for the road:

1. At the rise of the hand of the policeman, stop rapidly. Do not pass him, otherwise disrespect him.
2. When passenger of the foot heave in sight, tootle the horn trumpet melodiously at first, If he still obstacles your passage, tootle with vigor and express by word of mouth the warning "Hai. Hai."
3. Beware of the wandering horse that he shall not take fright as you pass him. Do not explosion the exhaust pipe. Go soothingly by him or stop by the roadside till he pass away.
4. Give big space to the festive dog that make sport in the roadway. Avoid entanglement with your wheel spoke.
5. Go soothingly on the grease mud as there lurk the skid demon.
6. Press the brake of the foot as you roll around the corner to save the collapse and tires up.

Here is a string of additional Japanese pearls:

► Be considerate—think for others.

► Artistic barber for cutting off of head.

► No horse back riding except in carriages.

► Outside a bar: Yo Come In. Yo Love Our Girls/And No Sheet-Keecking Music!

► Notice pasted on a door: Shut Up.

A notice in a Madras, India, newspaper proclaimed, "Our editors are colleged and write like the Kipling and the Dickens." *The Moscow Times* ran an ad under the heading INTERPRETING that advised, "Let us your letter of business translation do. Every people in our staffing know English like the hand of their back. Up to the min-uet wise-street phrases, don't you know, old boy." With instruction like this, it's no surprise that globe-trotting blooper snoopers uncover exotic jewels like the fol-lowing:

▶ *In a Sarajevo hotel:* Guests should announce abandon-ment of their rooms before 12 o'clock, emptying the room at the latest until 14 o'clock for the use of the room before 5 at the arrival or after the 16 o'clock at the departure will be billed as one more night.

▶ *In a hotel in Weifang, China:* Invisible service is avail-able for your rest being not disturbed.

▶ *In a Polish hotel:* The lock of our hotel room is efficient and warranting the safety. Pressing the handle in the room means that the door are open but nobody out-side can not open your room. We wish you pleasant stay and secure against attack.

▶ *From a hotel brochure in Qingdao, China:* Hua Tian Hotel is among the few best foreign affairs hotels.

▶ *In the brochure of an Italian hotel in the Dolomites area:* Standing among savage scenery, the hotel offers stu-pendous revelations. There is a French widow in every room. We can offer you a commodious cham-ber, with balcony imminent to a romantic gorge. We hope you want to drop in. In the close village you can buy jolly memorials for when you pass away.

▶ *In a brochure promoting a Sorrento, Italy, hotel:* Syrene Bellevue Hotel joins a modern functional equipment with a distinguished and smart style of the 18th century. It is located on the sea, far off the centre a few minutes afoot and owing to a number of gardens and sunny terraces, guarantee is given for an ideal stay in stillness and absolute rest. The restaurant salon with a large view of the Gulf of Naples, a restaurant service with a big choice, the private beach to be reached by a lift from inside directly, complete the undiscussable peculiarities of this unit.

▶ *In the English translation of a Spanish menu:* This joyful union of comestibles, chefs, and grateful appetites, holds as a stage this grand restaurant Don José, which dedicates itself to be the temple of the new racionalist religion called gastronomy. Intending to convert itself as the required pilgrimage for the great lovers of excellent cuisine.

▶ *At the front desk of a fancy Acapulco hotel:* If you presume to be in a hurry the day of your departure, ask our Front Desk personnel information about our Express Check Out.

▶ *From a Venezuelan travel brochure:* In this Expedition you will know the highets waterfall in the world. From Canaima, through the Sabana, the Jungle and the rivers Carrao & Churun, you'll enjoy one of the biggets emotions of this life. All the facilities Camp. Guides as natives, all experts, will bring you trough troubles waters, just where a few have made it. Be you one of them. Meals in open fire never taste so goo.

▶ *From a China Southwest Airlines in-flight magazine:* Not drink tea just after dieting. Otherwise, the tea will dilute gastric juice and play down digestion. While, the tannate of the tea will turn protein to a coagulum that uneasy to digest. This will heavy the bear of stomach. So, you would better drink tea one hour after dieting.

► *On a "Family Style" restaurant in Hong Kong:* Come Broil Yourself at Your Own Table.

► *On a Chinese menu:* Mr. Zheng and his fellowworkers like to meet you and entertain you with their hostility and unique cooking techniques.

► *On another Chinese menu:* Special cocktails for women with nuts.

► *On a Greek menu:* Spleen omelet, fisherman's crap soup, calf pluck, bowels.

► *On a Budapest menu:* Special today—no ice cream.

► *Outside a Mexico City disco:* Members and Non-Members Only

► *Sign on a ferry in San Juan harbor:* In case of emergency, the lifeguards are under the seat in the center of the vessel.

► *In a German pamphlet:* Our ETERNA Fountain-Pen is a revolting invention.

► *In a jeweler's window in India:* We shoot earholes.

► *In a Chinese in-flight magazine:* The stewardesses of Southwest Airlines must go through four steps, such as hardship, tiredment, dirt feeling. Beside the quality of general stewardess.

Like you, I chuckle at these skewed idioms and absurdly literal translations and wonder if foreign speakers of English are erecting a veritable Tower of Babble. On the other hand, I know that their English is a lot better than my Japanese, Chinese, Italian, Spanish, Polish, and German.

What do you call a person who speaks three languages? Trilingual. What do you call a person who speaks two languages? Bilingual. And what do you call a person who speaks one language? American.

I commend our foreign friends for making the effort at elegant expression in English and thank them from the heart of my bottom.

Brand New Bloopers

Come out of the grave with Pepsi.

A gourmet coffee was sold in Tokyo as an antidote to stress. Its name in English was intended to indicate that the product would soothe the troubled breast. Thus, the manufacturer chose Ease Your Bosoms.

The Japanese possess a special talent for concocting goofy brand names:

▶ A Gatorade-style sports drink called Pocari Sweat

▶ A line of stylish trousers called Trim Pecker

▶ A lawn fertilizer called Green Piles

- ▶ A nondairy creamer called Creap
- ▶ A candy called Carap
- ▶ A soft drink called Calpis
- ▶ Chocolates in a Band-Aid–style box called Hand-Maid Queer Aids
- ▶ A fingernail cleaner called Nail Remover

Other brand names that don't sell well in English-speaking markets include a canned spicy pepper sauce from Ghana named Shitto, a French soft drink called Pschitt, and a Finnish product used to unfreeze car locks called Super Piss.

The Germans named one of their products Merdol. They found they couldn't sell it in France.

The original ad slogan that the Swedes used for their Electrolux vacuum cleaner was "Nothing Sucks Like Electrolux!"

In Seoul, South Korea, the government received so many complaints about taxi drivers that it had to set up a telephone hotline for passengers who encountered rudeness or dangerous driving. To advise customers of this service, a sign was posted on the inside rear door of cabs, notifying English-speaking passengers of the availability of an "Intercourse Discomfort Report Center."

We laugh at such clumsy translations, yet we don't realize how equally susceptible we English speakers and writers are. Despite endless boardroom cogitation, many a multinational corporation has ended up with its brand name or slogan on its face. Global slip-ups remind us that few words and idioms can be literally translated. *Caveat vendor*—seller beware: it's best to hire the best for translation.

More than others, the automobile industry seems to be prone to linguistic accidents. The classic story of vehicular misnaming is associated with General Motors. As the literal translation of the brand name Nova to Spanish means "star," why then, GM wanted to know, were Hispanic Chevrolet dealerships so unaccommodating to this model? That's because, when spoken aloud, Nova sounds like *no va*—which means, "it doesn't go." GM changed the name to Caribe.

Ford Motor Company's Caliente turned out to mean "streetwalker" in Mexico. Ford came up with a second flat tire in Japan, where Cortina translated as "jalopy." The company discovered that a truck model it called Fiera means "ugly old woman" in Spanish. As if this was not enough, it turns out that Pinto is a slang term meaning "small male appendage."

Even the luxurious Rolls-Royce Company found out the hard way that in German, Silver Mist means "human waste."

Here are more classic cross-border marketing misfortunes that got lost in translation:

▶ The colas of the world have been shaken up explosively by mistranslation. When Pepsi-Cola invaded the huge Chinese and German markets, the effort initially fizzled. The product's slogan, "Come alive with the Pepsi generation," was rendered (or should I say rent?) into Chinese as "Pepsi brings back your dead ancestors" and into German as "Come out of the grave with Pepsi."

▶ Coca-Cola also discovered in Taiwan that the Chinese characters chosen to sound like its name mean "Bite the wax tadpole." Coke then changed to a set of characters that mean "Happiness in the mouth."

▶ Fresca's brand name fizzled in Mexico, where its name turned out to be slang for "lesbian."

▶ When Coors Beer cast its slogan, "Turn It Loose," in Spanish the statement read as "Suffer from diarrhea."

▶ Perdue chicken's slogan "It takes a tough man to make a tender chicken" read, in Spanish, "It takes a sexually stimulated man to make a chicken affectionate."

▶ Braniff Air Lines, promoting its comfortable leather seats, used the headline *"Sentado en cuero,"* which was interpreted as "Sit naked."

▶ Clairol hair products introduced its Mist Stick curling iron in Germany only to find that *mist* is German slang for "manure." Germans did not stand in long lines waiting to buy Manure Sticks.

▶ 3M translated its Scotch tape slogan, "Sticks like crazy," into Japanese and came up with a sticky problem. The slogan translated literally into Japanese as "It sticks foolishly."

▶ Kellogg encountered a problem when it introduced its Bran Buds to Sweden. The name translates loosely into Swedish as Burnt Farmer.

▶ Vicks had to change its product name to Wicks before entering the German market when it was discovered that Vicks sounded like a vulgar verb in German.

▶ Not to be outdone, Puffs tissues found that *Puff* in German is a colloquial term for a whorehouse.

▶ Parker Pen's Jotter ballpoint pen could not be marketed with that name in some Latin countries because *jotter* happens to be slang for "jockstrap."

▶ Colgate Palmolive had to discard Cue as the name for its toothpaste in France. *Cue* is the name of a widely circulated French pornographic magazine.

Even the wrong nonverbal cue can play hob with a product's reception in a far-off land:

▶ Gerber baby food initially packaged their African product just the same as in the United States—with a cute baby picture on the jar. They didn't realize that because so many Africans cannot read, nearly all packaged products sold in Africa carry pictures of what is inside. Puréed baby—horrors!

▶ Muslims in Bangladesh rioted and ransacked Thom McAn stores when they mistook the company's logo on some sandals for the Arabic letters for Allah. One person was killed and 50 people were injured before the melee ended.

Misdirected Directions

When the Basic Time corresponds to the preset Alarm Time, the alarm is generated. If you have a depress on 'snooze' while it is alarmed, the loud will stop immediately and loud for another 8 minutes after having this 'snooze' 8 minutes and so on. However, alarm will not effect if it has lasted for fully 8 minutes unless the second correspondence that is to say after 24 hours.

Watch out for a new crisis: imported English. Many foreign products are worth the price, if only for the instructions. My fellow Americans, we need protection, if not protectionism, against these assaults from abroad on our English language.

A portable fan made in Hong Kong "has been realised in a way to solve the problem of an exceptional practicality." On the box is written the injunction to "unscrew the lamp and screw your small fan."

The instructions accompanying a humidifier made in Japan warn, "Avoiding wind blowing directly to human body at a long period of time. Especial for patient, childern, drunken, and people with heart disease."

Here is a catalog of misdirected directions that get lost in translation. All spelling and syntax are reproduced exactly as printed:

▶ Washing instructions for a track suit manufactured in Bangladesh: Impregnation after wash is recommended.

▶ Selected instructions for the use of the washer/dryer in a Spanish youth hostel:

AUTOMATIC SELF-SERVICE
CLOTHES WASHING AND DRYING

The direction of this establishment, with the purpose to make your stay more comfortable, offers you a clothes washing and drying self-service. We wish this service make your stay here more pleasant.—The Direction

Put the detergent in the bottom of the machine and don't get your clothes in bend and tight.

Don't put in metallic objects neither shoes. Your clothes can be spoilt.

Shut the cover, introduce the chip, and move the purse down to the bottom, and get it back to the inicial position.

If the red light of unstable starts to shine, get up the cover and distribute uniformently the clothes.

Consult in reception the machines situation.

▶ On the back of a Korean "New Adhesion Fuzz Roller," one of those permanently sticky lint and hair removers:

How to Use It
  1. Pulling to the arrow direction, the cover will be open.

2. Stripe off the transparent vinyl cover the adhesion-roll.
3. With the rolling action back and forth, the dust is absorbed.
4. Deserve it inside its cover after use it.

Warning

As it is used by washing repeatedly roll without exchange: Suit, Sweater, Carpet, Sofa, Cushion, Car seat, and cover, Dust or thread of handcrafts, The fur of pet, etc.

Don't use it on the plastic file or glass, because the roll is sticked to and separated from the body.

Don't use it to cleanse of the glass splinters or ceramics.

Keep it from the direct sunrays.

▶ From Taiwan swoops in the Waden Spring Magic Air Plane (Hand-Play is Available):

The method to fly the magic Airplane is different from the other conventional toy Airplanes flying horizontally.

1. Spring-Play Flying. Spring this Airplane to left (or right) hand and it can fly back circularly from reverse direction.
2. Spring it 45 degrees downward and it can fly back circularly from upward direction.
3. Spring is upward and it can roll and go back from rest direction.

HAND-PLAY FLYING: The best fly is to extend our arm holding the metal clamp on the Airplane head diagonally with the Airplane wing vertically against the ground then throw it right or left hand direction.

▶ For a paper-and-plastic model glider kit manufactured in Romania:

1. Matching weight balance, and toss 5 or 7 angle down direction.
2. Right flying as the picture 1 shown.
3. Remove back fore wing when bouncing fore-head up, and then get it down as the picture 2 shown.
4. Remove forward fore wing when fore-head going downward on a sudden as the picture 3 shown.

▶ Writes a Damariscotta, Maine, reader, "A friend received this 'Stove Top Grill' three years ago at Christmas but has been unable to figure out the Korean directions and has, therefore, never used it":

Please use the holding dish after pouring water in.

In case of use for the first time it is necessary to be adopted with the edible on the surface of the plate upon a little warmed up.

Please avoid heating with empty or excessive heating.

Taking cares after use should use water or detergent of table wares and wash with soft sponge. Please avoide use of cleanser or metal scrubbing brush.

▶ From a Chinese manufacturer of alarm clocks:

When the Basic Time corresponds to the preset Alarm Time, the alarm is generated. The Alarm tune will automatically cease after 1 minute working. If you have a depress on 'SNOOZE' while it is alarmed, the loud will stop immediately and loud for another 8 minutes after having this 'SNOOZE' 8 minutes and so on. However, alarm will not effect if it has lasted for fully 8 minutes unless the second correspondence that is to say after 24 hours.

▶ Clients of a Hong Kong manufacturer some years ago

took delivery of an electric compressor, to which was attached the following "Instruction and Guarantee Card":

1. This is an excellent equipment with very few noise and excessive reliability. Though unfragile, it is also robust, and should not be belted.
2. Circuit arrangements ensure environments, and imput current is best at both temperatures, including snow and hot.
3. Stability is too good on full battery and this should be lowered, but the imput may be reduced to danger level if preferred.
4. The negative will be and the positive is not if supply polarity is incorrect; also a humming noise will be introduced together with smoke. When setting up, the best angle has no smoke and slight smell.
5. When aligning, twiddle for strong current and prevent sparks.
6. The motor should be good for ever, but pregnant wear-out may occur after a few summers if heat is applied.

DO NOT DOUBT THE GUARANTEE. IT IS BACKED BY MANY YEARS IN HONG KONG WITHOUT ODOUR, PATIENCE, OR THREAT.

Loopy instructions are also manufactured right here in America. Here are a few examples of homemade gibberish:

► Take 1 Teaspoonful 4 times a day. Swish and spit. Do not swallow for 10 days.

► We Make It! You Bake It! Pizza. Why call & wait 30 minutes for a pizza to be delivered when you can

Take-N-Bake from Buscemis. Take home & cook yourself in 10 minutes fresh out of your own oven.

▶ Instructions for a golf tournament: Closest-to-the-pin
competition. Measure your distance quickly and record on the clipboard at the green. While you are
doing this, the rest of your group can be putting out.

Mrs. Malaprop Lives!

"I'm calling on my cellulite phone."

More than 200 years ago, Mrs. Malaprop first bustled onto the stage, her nouns whirling, her verbs twirling, her adjectives swirling. Mrs. Malaprop, you may recall from high-school English, was the "old weather-beaten she-dragon" in Richard Brinsley Sheridan's *The Rivals*. Malaprop took special pride in her use of the king's English: "Sir, if I reprehend anything in this world, it is the use of my oracular tongue and a nice derangement of epitaphs!" What a shame, she lamented, that so few gentlemen "know how to value the ineffectual qualities in a woman!"

The delightful dowager was such "a pineapple of perfection" of her type that her name has come to stand for the confused and befuddling misapplication of words. Nowadays a malapropism means the replacement of a big word with another that often has a parallel but unintended sense.

Some people will insist that Mrs. Malaprop was merely a creature of the dramatic imagination. But I am here to tell you that people like her actually exist. You may be one of them, or married to one of them, or friends with one of them, or work with one of them.

"I stand before this court chaste," an O. J. Simpson defense lawyer told Judge Lance Ito. He meant *chastened*, of course.

A letter describing the "new navy" included this incentive: "Then there are the free medical benefits and low-cost insurance. And travel to foreign ports—with 30 days' paid vacation to see and enjoy these erotic places."

The West Virginia legislature passed a law forbidding "the picking of flora or fauna within 100 yards of a highway."

A news photo pictured a woman walking around an old cemetery in San Antonio, Texas. The caption read: "Judy Fisher reviews these hollowed grounds."

Because they are the very pineapple of verbal foe paws, I receive more malapropisms from my contributors than any other kind of gaffe:

▶ In Venice, the people travel around the canals on gargonzolas.

▶ In the United States, people are put to death by elocution.

▶ The two sides in a court trial are the defense and the prostitution.

▶ I haven't seen him in over a year. I hear he went to one of those ivory league colleges.

▶ Okay, ma'am, I'm going to give you a ballpoint figure.

▶ Isn't Rogaine the stuff that if you apply it tropically, you can grow hair?

▶ I didn't like the writer because he was sarcastic with a pestamistic view of life.

▶ The church service was so beautiful it was positively urethral.

▶ She's led a sedimentary life.

▶ The sponge was very exorbitant.

▶ He's always hurling epitaphs at people.

▶ I can't advise you on this, so use your own discrepancy.

▶ My check bounced because of insignificant funds.

▶ Remember that the participation of all CCHS members is detrimental to our success!

▶ When the Martians' spaceship landed, they got out and had testicles all over their heads.

▶ The food in our cafeteria is so bad it's not fit for human constipation.

▶ The Alberta Pipeline was largely financed through private investigators.

▶ Freud constructed the Edifice complex, Vienna's first shopping mall.

▶ In families with incest, there seems to be a marked

dispurity in the amount of power held by the man and the wife.

▶ He was arrested for parking tickets and other mister meaners.

▶ In a university commencement program: The audience is asked to remain seated until the end of the recession.

▶ In America the elderly are often whorehoused.

▶ I've got Elvis records up the kazoo.

▶ I was so hungry I was absolutely ravished.

▶ A Spanish Armada ship sank years ago off the coast of Florida. When I lived there, divers would search the wreckage for gold bunions.

▶ Many college students are abscessed with TV.

▶ In the afternoon, I like to lay on my bed, rest, and watch the so-poppers.

▶ President Clinton was a Road Scholar.

▶ Adultery is what adolescents are practicing for.

▶ I want that list arranged in condescending order.

▶ Children tend to put their parents on a petal stool.

▶ The pirate leaped upon the deck with a cut glass at his side.

▶ The British Museum was a millstone in the development of civilization.

► I plead the fifth commandment.

► I drank myself into Bolivia.

► I'm calling on my cellulite phone.

► I'm blessed with a photogenic memory.

► Game canceled due to inclimate weather.

► I offer this solution to the problem that plagiarizes all of us.

► This looks just like the American deadly lampshade.

► He suffered from low self of steam.

► You're hand stringing my creativity.

► I am utterly dumbfolded.

► Our daughter got an A in suppository writing.

► Children so smart they are in exhilarated classes.

► Several workers were laid off, but they all received sufferance pay.

► I can give you the recipe for my fruit compost.

► Now it might get a little cool tonight, so just pull that African at the foot of the bed over you.

► Her ex-husband received a decease-and-desist order.

► A few members argue that it would be a mute point if the majority doesn't speak out.

► She digressed back to her childhood.

► I refuse to answer on the grounds that it may incinerate me.

▶ There's no astigmatism attached to that.

▶ My contact lenses adhere to the contortions of my eye.

▶ The decimal level was too high to measure.

▶ She was dressed in full regatta.

▶ I have a good rappaport with just about everyone.

▶ This letter is to memorialize our telephone conversation of October 22nd.

▶ This list is impartial. I need a complete list.

▶ This will only exasperate the problem.

▶ We hired a new salesman because we were so underhanded.

▶ It was a real cliff-dweller.

▶ His attendance has been very erotic.

▶ The museum contains many artifacts and pimentos of the past.

▶ Make your homecoming a memorial one.

▶ They attend the Conjugal Church.

▶ Meanwhile, the state has already spent the money collected from the exuberant fee.

▶ My son's grades have taken a real nosedrop.

▶ I'm taking desecrated liver tablets.

▶ After the service, entertainment will follow at the local cemetery.

▶ The world today is full of crime and phonography.

▶ I don't believe in heaven or hell, but I do believe in puberty.

When Metaphors Collide

You can't change the spots on an old dog.

"The Communist menace is a snake in the grass that is gnawing away at the foundation of our ship of state" is a classic mixed metaphor from a University of Chicago student's essay.

"You're biting the hand of the goose that laid the golden egg," Hollywood mogul Sam Goldwyn once Goldwynized.

Chicago mayor Harold Washington carved out a niche of his own in the Mixed Metaphor Hall of Shame when he explained to the local press the objective of his planned news conferences: "It has been our purpose all along to have a sort of a periodical potpourri to cover all of this flotsam and jetsam that flies through the media that can get nailed down on a regular, periodic track. So, in a sense, that can be interpreted as open sesame, but don't throw darts."

I never metaphor I didn't like, and I never met a mixed metaphor I didn't collect. I now grab the bull by the tail and present the cream of the dregs of figures of speech that just don't add up:

▶ Hillary Clinton's ratings are dropping through the roof.

▶ Senator Dole is off on the wrong foot in a head-to-head comparison with President Clinton.

▶ Detroit Pistons star Grant Hill praised his new coach, Doug Collins, for his drive: "It's a fire that starts at the top and trickles its way back down."

▶ The inimitable Robert J. Lurtsema, music host on Boston public radio, introduced a collection of new phonograph records just received, by saying, "We've just barely begun to scratch the surface of this new set of records."

▶ Answering a reporter's question, an interviewee opined that not paying federal workers for time missed in a government shutdown was "the only way to get President Clinton to hold his seat to the fire."

▶ What with all this new technology, Newtown is standing on the verge of a minefield of opportunity.

▶ Let's jump right in and get our teeth wet.

▶ That's water under the dam.

▶ Let's not stir up sleeping dogs.

▶ We've just scratched the tip of the iceberg.

▶ Let's be sure that the contract covers all the asses.

▶ My new Saab is unbelievable. It's the Cadillac of cars.

▶ For too long the Prime Minister has been sitting on the fence with both ears to the ground as part of his play-safe political style.

▶ The light at the end of the tunnel is just the tip of the iceberg.

▶ This is the story of a boy who wore his buck teeth like a chip on his shoulder.

▶ I've got an ace up my hole.

▶ He was bleeding like a stuffed pig.

▶ That was the last straw on the camel's back.

▶ I'm drinking enough soup to float a battle-ax.

▶ You can't change the spots on an old dog.

▶ She put her head between her tail and apologized.

▶ We had some disagreements early in her career but she's turned her attitude around 360 degrees since then.

▶ Raines spearheads Whales Alive, one of several non-profit organizations dedicated to saving the world's whale population.

▶ There's so much going on at work, I can barely keep my feet above water.

▶ It was like pulling hens' teeth.

▶ You're dead meat in the water.

▶ Separate the wheat from the shaft.

▶ The pianist has the fastest fingers ever to set foot on stage.

▶ The underground parking garage will never see the light of day.

▶ The worm is on the other foot.

▶ It's time to fish or get off the pot.

▶ John Brown fired the shot that set the ball rolling right up to the gates of the Civil War.

▶ I wouldn't eat it with a 10-foot pole.

▶ If you jump the gun in the realty business, you can end up with egg on your face.

▶ He smokes like a fish.

▶ If the hand were on the other foot . . .

▶ I let my hair down and got it off my chest.

▶ Remember, she's no fried chicken.

▶ Bob Dole praised President Clinton for fielding a flood of questions about Whitewater.

▶ I hope in my next life I can be a government official so that I can feather my own pockets for a change.

▶ This is a clear case of the cart wagging the donkey.

▶ What can I do? I'm only a big wheel in a small pond.

▶ This field of research is so virginal that no human eyeball has ever set foot on it.

▶ I don't mind having my feet to the fire. My problem is that I've got so many balls in the air.

▶ Her leg was amputated after a long-standing illness.

▶ In our family we bend over backward to be upright and honest.

▶ Oral sex is distasteful.

▶ I made out like a banshee.

▶ Let's get down to brass tactics.

▶ It's a Pandora's box hanging over our heads.

▶ We are on parallel tracks that are unlikely to cross over since they are divergent.

▶ The future is an uncharted sea full of potholes.

▶ The matrimonial agency was barely making ends meet.

▶ The diving school was barely keeping its head above water.

▶ Let's try, by a process of elimination, to discover what caused your diarrhea.

▶ We're back to square zero.

▶ A wedding aboard a luxurious cruise boat can run from $3,000 to $20,000, if someone wants to go overboard.

▶ The chasms in my general knowledge are abysmal.

▶ I was way out on third base.

▶ He was three shades in the wind.

▶ She was born with a silver slipper in her mouth.

▶ She has more jewelry than you can shake a cat at.

▶ You've got to put your foot down with a firm hand.

► What can you do when you're at the bottom of the rung?

► You've hit the iceberg on the head.

► They're trying to pull the wool over my face.

► I'm not mending bridges we've already sold down the river.

► With our new fall line, we're going to plummet right to the top.

► They're coming out of the wormwood.

► I only have two pair of hands.

► Let's bite the bull by the horns.

► He's foaming at the bit.

► Treat him with golden gloves.

► This is where the rubber hits the road. This is the kickoff, not the end product. We're throwing down the gauntlet.

And from *The Acting President*, by Bob Schieffer and Gary Paul Gates: "He could not shake the feeling that he and all the others who had been involved in those projects were sitting on a bomb that, sooner or later, would explode in their faces."

How's That Again?

I don't think people realize how difficult it is to be a pawn of labor.

Dear Son:

I am writing this letter slowly because I know you can't read fast. We no longer live where we did when you left. Your dad read in the paper that most accidents happen within 20 miles of home, so we moved. I won't be able to send you the address because the last family that lived here took the house numbers with them so they wouldn't have to change their address.

This place has a washing machine. The first day,

I put four shirts in it, pulled down the handle, and haven't seen them since.

The coat you wanted me to send you—Aunt Sue said it would be too heavy to send in the mail with all those big buttons on it. So I cut them off and put them in the pocket.

It rained twice this week, three days the first time and four days the second time.

Your sister had a baby this morning. I don't know if it was a boy or a girl, so I don't know if you are an uncle or an aunt.

I was going to send you some money, but the envelope was already sealed.

Love,
Your mother

P.S. Hope you get this letter. If you don't, let me know.

As much as this folk-letter tears logic to tatters, there are plenty of real-life examples that match it, non sequitur for non sequitur.

The Illinois Department of Public Aid sent the following letter to a dead person: "Beginning in February 1976 your assistance benefits will be discontinued. Reason: it has been reported to our office that you expired on January 1, 1976. May God bless you. You may reapply if there is a change in your circumstances."

An obituary in a Peoria, Illinois, newspaper read: "Mr. Martin Shore was born in Madison, Wisconsin, where he died and later moved to Peoria."

During the Vietnam War, a U.S. military officer explained, "We had to destroy that town in order to save it."

On a widely used jury qualification questionnaire is

printed this question: "Do you read, speak, and understand English? Yes ☐ No ☐."

Near Warrenton, Virginia, stand two signs that redefine the meaning of *trespassing*. At a construction site is placed a warning that reads: NO UNAUTHORIZED TRESPASSING ALLOWED. I didn't know that there was such a thing as authorized trespassing. A sign on a country store in the same area advises: NO TRESPASSING AFTER 10 P.M. Apparently trespassing before 10 P.M. is perfectly all right.

Actor Dennis Hopper sagely observed, "After the eighties, the nineties will make the fifties look like the sixties." Quite so.

A husband and wife were watching a television show she had taped. The wife kept getting up during the commercial breaks to do chores and hurrying back each time the program resumed.

The husband asked, "Have you forgotten that this show is on tape? You can fast-forward through the commercials."

Her reply: "If I don't work during the commercials, I'll never get anything done."

A woman explained how she continued to get involved with men who abused her. She would break free from one and promptly get involved with another who would beat her. "I swear, I wouldn't know a good man if he came up and hit me on the head," she lamented.

The sagacious Hobbes, of the late comic strip *Calvin and Hobbes,* once predicted that "we can eventually make language a complete impediment to understanding." Hobbes had it just about right when it comes to statements such as the following:

▶ Perhaps the most cruel tragedy in the death yesterday of Caleb Witherspoon is that had it happened a few minutes later, he might still be alive.

▶ The Pharmacology Unit seeks healthy male or female volunteers, who have had a hysterectomy, tubal ligation, or are at least three years past menopause, to participate in a research study.

▶ The most common surgery in America today is total hysterectomy, and operations for women are more common than those for men.

▶ I'll tell you one thing. He always ceases to amaze me!

▶ Sign on the men's room door at the offices of the Detroit School Board: Please keep the door closed when coming in or going out.

▶ Label on a bag of dry cat food: $1/2$ Lb. More Than Other 3.5 Lb. Bags.

▶ Instructions on a paper-towel dispenser: Pull down. Tear up.

▶ Store ad: Semi-Annual Clearance Sale
               Once-In-A-Lifetime Opportunity

▶ A Denver TV channel offered this sage advice: "Don't go into darkened parking lots unless they are well lighted."

▶ Newfoundland is a very small island, but its size is bigger on land.

▶ The dead live in the cemetery.

▶ I don't think people realize how difficult it is to be a pawn of labor.

▶ We're launching a new innovation for the first time.

▶ We can't make good grammar great. But we want to make flawed writing acceptable.

▶ If you missed seeing Desmond Morris's *The Human Animal* the first time, now you can see it again.

▶ Your subscription is about to expire, and delivery will stop. Please send payment now to avoid uninterrupted delivery.

▶ After finding no qualified candidates for the position of principal, the school department is extremely pleased to announce the appointment of Arthur Harrison to the post.

▶ A bachelor's life is no life for a single man.

▶ Closed for official opening.

▶ Wood doesn't grow on trees, you know.

▶ You have no idea what a poor opinion I have of myself, and how little I deserve it.
　　—W. S. Gilbert

▶ Boys, elevate them guns a little lower.
　　—Andrew Jackson at the battle of New Orleans

▶ You gotta remember—nobody's human.

▶ Annual Polish Day Picnic—Sunday September 8 & 9.

▶ Working together to solve a problem with the result not only resolving the initial problem but improving it as well.

▶ Display ad for a monster movie: Due to the horrifying nature of this film, no one will be admitted to the theater.

▶ Label found on the bottom of a wind-up kitchen timer: Do not place on or near heat-producing appliances.

▶ Inscription on a bathroom scale: Permanently Adjusted.

▶ WEATHER FORECAST—Thunder showers Friday probably followed by Saturday.

▶ Law office advertisement: Permanent Injuries Last a Lifetime.

▶ At a health center: Prescriptions required the following day must be handed in the day before.

▶ Mr. Garver will remain Director of the Company throughout the end of the fiscal year, except in the event of his death, in which case he will no longer be Director of the Company.

▶ Two-dimensional photographs simply don't do this car justice.

▶ Killing an animal while it is still alive is unacceptable.

▶ There is a fundamental difference between male and female homosexuality, which is that the former concerns men and the second women.

▶ Standing at the casket of her husband, who was mangled in a car wreck, a grieving widow said, "Oh, God, he'd die if he knew he looked like that!"

▶ The most important thing in acting is honesty. Once you've learned to fake it, you're in.

▶ A mother warned her son: "If you climb that tree and fall out, don't come running to me!"

▶ 21% of girls left because they had become a mother, as did 8% of the boys.

▶ Dates from Zafarraya Cave, Spain, indicate that Neanderthals lived millennia longer than once believed.

V

MECHANICAL BREAKDOWNS

Under a Spell

ESCAPEE CAPTURED AFTER 10 DAYS ON THE LAMB.

Because of economic conditions, a famous English private school was obliged to raise its tuition. A letter informing parents of this fact stated that the increase would be 500 £ per annum, except unfortunately it was spelled *per anum.* An irate parent wrote to the headmaster, thanking him for the notification but saying, "For my part, I would prefer to continue paying through the nose, as usual."

A similar error occurred when the *Los Angeles Times* reported that 1992 was a fiery year for the royal family in England. It was a year of flame-ups, flame-outs, new flames, and just plain flamers among her family: fire in Windsor Castle and tremendous marital shake-ups. Quoting Queen Elizabeth II, the *Times* reported that "the queen said that the year had been an *anus horribilis*." Considering what had happened, one would certainly have to agree.

A friend and fellow word watcher stopped to buy some writing supplies in Kansas City and noticed that the gold-lettered sign in the window read STATIONARY STORE.

She pointed this out to the woman behind the counter and explained, "That one means immobile, unmoving, in one place."

"Well, honey," said the clerk as she counted out the change, "we've been at this location for 17 years."

A geography quiz question asked: What's the oldest desert in the world? Wrote one student: apple pie.

A transplant from northern California got a taste of Utah culture when he ordered a cake from a Salt Lake City grocery store for his wife's fiftieth birthday. He requested this inscription: IT'S BETTER TO BE 50 THAN PREGNANT. When he picked up the cake, the inscription read: IT'S BETTER TO BE 50 THEN PREGNANT.

A New Jersey woman hired a desktop publisher to make invitations for her birthday celebration. It wasn't until after they were mailed that she noticed the error:

Grace Mortonson
Requests Your Presents
For Her
40th Birthday Party

Mark Twain once wrote, "I don't see any use in having a uniform and arbitrary way of spelling words. We might as well make all clothing alike and cook all dishes alike.

Sameness is tiresome, variety is pleasure. *Kow* spelled with a large *K* is just as good as with a small *c.* It is better. It gives the imagination a broader field, a wider scope."

Andrew Jackson, who may have been our only illiterate president, once thundered, "It's a damn small mind that can think of only one way to spell a word!"

Twain and Jackson would be delighted with the creativity and broad-mindedness shown in the misspellings that follow. They certainly fill the imagination with all sorts of original images. As a famous bumper sticker proclaims, BAD SPELLERS OF THE WORLD, UNTIE!

▶ Meanwhile, Richard Parker Bowles, brother of Camilla's ex-husband, Andrew, said that from the beginning Camilla approved of Charles's marrying Diana while she remained his power mower.

▶   Only Worn Once
        Wedding Dress for Sale
   Victorian style, ecru lace, long sleeves,
  high neck, drop-waste tea-length, size 10

▶ Volunteers needed for the Grater Indianapolis Literacy League.

▶ Nationally reknown literary consultant. There is no substitute for excellence.

▶ The Production Department is looking for a part-time proofreader. This person must be proficient in spelling grammer and punctuation, able to work on their own, as well as with a team of salespeople and production staff.

▶ The Home Education Association invites your organization to be a part of the Annual Cirriculum Fair.

▶ Microsoft Word advertisement: You'll get a grammer checker and a spelling checker.

- ▶ Need to be a better reader? John Atkinson is available as a reading tudor.

- ▶ Congratulations to all 1st graders who participated in the annual Spelling Be.

- ▶ Congradulations to our school's champion spelers.

- ▶ Say "yes" to eduction.

- ▶ FOR SALE. Two-story 1500 sq. ft. on 2 acres with privacy fencing along road frontage. On hill with beautiful view of damned creek below property.

- ▶ ATTENTION MEMBERS: During the week of December 14th, the pool will be painted with an epoxy paint. There will be fumes in the club. Please bare with us.

- ▶ No smoking aloud.

- ▶ The prisoner was sent to solitaire confinement.

- ▶ An inspired Illinois team yesterday reached the pinochle of success.

- ▶ Children waded in the clear blue-green waters yesterday while fishermen stood waste-high in the calm current, casting and reeling.

- ▶ Taped to a cash register in a convenience store:
    No Checks Excepted!
    No Acceptions!

- ▶ FOR SALE: String of perils, 30 years old, with box.

- ▶ She arrived at the castle and spent the knight.

- ▶ He was a short, fat, semi-balled man.

- ▶ I believe in family values too, but I'm really annoyed by the oblique view of abortion. I don't think it's an issue that belongs in government. We're back to ar-

guing morals and morays that belong in church discussions.

▶ Mrs. Travis unveiled a plague in memory of her late
husband.

▶ Escapee captured after 10 days on the lamb

▶ Wedding gown: Satin with sequence & beading.

▶ He killed the men with his bear hands.

▶ Six years ago Vinny Testaverde played catch with a
toe-headed high school kid.

▶ You'll have the special facts you need to analize the
market.

▶ She slipped into a comma on Thursday.

▶ Church Bizarre Sale. Refreshments. Saturday, June 24.
9 a.m.

▶ On the menu of a Rockford, Illinois, restaurant:
Toasted Beagal and Cream Cheese.

▶ He went to the carnival and rode on the fairest wheel.

▶ The weather was wonderful and the little boy did
summer salts.

▶ Divorce has become so common that we take it with
a grain assault.

▶ A story in a Florida newspaper quoted a minister as
saying, "God told me to hold my piece."

▶ I stood on the beach as the serf blew in my face.

▶ He was arrested for evading an officer and for wreck-
less driving.

- When his Gravol injection was due, he was found coward in the corner wretching.

- In order to ensure safety, all our cars are fitted with duel controls.

- He was best known for his pukish humor.

- Insanity is a problem of considerable dementions.

- Choice of dressing: Italian, Ranch, Blew Cheese.

- They unleashed the attack dogs that go for the juggler.

- Give Your Sweatheart a Dozen Roses for Valentine's Day.

- Bracelets $8.00
  Neckless $10.00

- While the car is a wreck, its occupants can be truly grateful that they escaped with their lives. The tree is badly scared.

- The woman's basketball team earned a birth in the finals.

- A girl bought a boot and ear for her boyfriend when they went to the prom.

- Platonic love is where you first love a single woman. Then you come to love women as a hole.

- It's better to slow down then get a ticket.

- A flaming desert complimented the dinner.

- No dumping aloud.

It's best to heed the advice of the *United Press International Stylebook:* "A burro is an ass. A burrow is a hole in the ground. As a writer, you are expected to know the difference."

Back to Grammar School

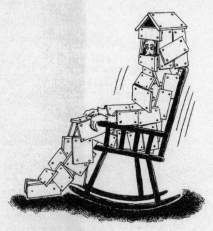

The house belongs to Martha Bender who is in a nursing home and has been boarded up for several years.

Many of us find that grammar gaffes are like chewing tinfoil, or like chalk squeaking over the blackboard of our sensibilities. The tinfoil is especially metallic and the chalk especially squeaky when the mistake is perpetrated by people who obviously should know better.

"Students don't have to fail. Exhilarated classes day or evening," claims one newspaper ad. "Develop interpersonal conversational skills by learning to talk good," boasts a second ad. "Can't tell *who* from *whom?* Help is available from the Lowe University grammar hotline. We get a lot of business-writing calls and how to deal with a

salutation when you don't know who you're writing to,''
a third points out.

No wonder teachers receive student evaluations like
these:

▶ While in the writing program, I learned a lot about
sentence structure, punctuation, and capitalism.

▶ I past all my testes. My grade should be hirer.

▶ I have learned a lot about life here at college. For in-
stance, I have learned to do minor household repairs
such as painting, fixing old windows, and replacing
old broads.

▶ Another thing I learned was way's to use apostrofe's
and where it goe's and sometime's not to use them.

▶ Your a fine teacher. I would recommend you at any
time.

Makes teaching all worthwhile, doesn't it?

Squeak! Squeak! Yikes! Yikes! Here are some more
grammar gaffes gouged into the blackboards of our
minds:

▶ Old Sedberghians are invited to a weekend reunion
at the school. We would like to extend a particularly
warm invitation to all of you who left Sedbergh and
your wives.

▶ The easiest hole on the course, Deb Richard found the
fairway bunker both times she played it.

▶ Two new booklets are available for South Carolinians
who are survivors of head injuries and their families.

▶ He was arrested Saturday, hours after the most recent

victim's body was discovered and questioned for 12 hours.

▶ Ms. Duncan distributed several door prizes at the conclusion of her talk, including a sample of jewelry made by craftspeople, meticulously lacquered to preserve them and make them safe.

▶ Many people have no respect for the American flag. I have seen them hanging from windows, dirty and sometimes torn.

▶ Gabriel Pincus is the proud possessor of a brand new Chevrolet sedan and also a new wife, having traded in the old one, for which he received a liberal allowance.

▶ I had an infection after the operation and was on antibiotics for two weeks before going home. There were still some minor pains in my testicles, but they disappeared.

▶ Mr. and Mrs. Crane Lauder, of Tennessee, are seeing their loved ones here. Dr. C. H. Karston removed Mr. Lauder's tonsils and they are now with his sister, Mrs. Peyton.

▶ If Ms. Hunter and Ms. Brown agree to relinquish ownership of the dogs, they will be euthanized.

▶ Joe Harrigan's father passed away yesterday from a massive heart attack. He won't be back in the office until Tuesday.

▶ It was called into the Burbury P.D. that a deer had been hit north of Gendry Bros. The deer is dead and he has locked himself out of the car and is waiting for a locksmith.

▶ And now for a look at the weather, made possible by Foam Shampoo.

▶ The house belongs to Martha Bender who is in a nursing home and has been boarded up for several years.

▶ A Groveton officer described the driver as a white male with blond hair, wearing shorts, a gray tank top and bare feet.

▶ All proceeds from the sale of carved ducks will go to handicap children.

▶ The bride carried a bouquet of spring blossoms as well as the three bridesmaids.

▶ Air piracy charges were filed Sunday against a man who used grenades to hijack a Russian airliner and his wife.

▶ Females should have the same athletic opportunities as males: it is an almost universal medical opinion that there is no sport more dangerous to a girl than a boy.

▶ Asphalt tennis courts are hard on the soles of the feet and balls.

Some of the most subtle errors are generated by poor punctuation. Note the havoc wreaked—and reeked—by a missing comma in this ad: "Lady desires post: domesticated, fond of cooking children."

Now consider the effect of a misplaced or missing apostrophe in these unexemplary examples:

▶ Police report that the man took a crescent wrench and swung it at one of the victim's heads.

▶ We sell children's clothes and babies too.

▶ WANTED: Guitar for college student to learn to play, also piano to replace daughters lost in fire.

Even the absence or misplacement of a hyphen can produce bizarre results:

▶ Museum staffer Jill Dorman checks out 65 million year-old eggs.

▶ Cases of Lyme disease, which is transmitted by deer-carrying ticks, are on the rise.

▶ CHILD ABUSING PRIEST TO FACE NEW CHARGES

That headline seems extremely weird until you read the story that follows: "A convicted pedophile priest is due to appear in court in Belfast next month to face new charges of child sex abuse."

Those Dang(ling) Modifiers

The Collier County sheriff's office has announced that one of its dog deputies has been named number one dog deputy for capturing a kidnap suspect after holding a female hostage for several hours.

Reading the following statements from newspaper stories, we may well ask ourselves what's going on in our courts these days:

▶ The juror never was asked if he had been molested by either defense or prosecution attorneys.

▶ Bernard Constantino pleaded guilty to charges of distributing marijuana Wednesday in front of Judge Hart.

▶ A homeless man accused of breaking into a whale watching boat on Rose's Wharf was ordered to receive inpatient treatment in the Plowshare program for his drinking problem in district court Monday.

▶ The Collier County sheriff's office has announced that one of its dog deputies has been named number one dog deputy for capturing a kidnap suspect after holding a female hostage for several hours.

▶ Grodskins was arrested for illegal consumption of alcohol by the sheriff's department on Sunday.

▶ Ms. Innes testified that the defendant was told by a child abuse specialist that her daughter was more than likely being sexually abused in Belknap County Superior Court.

▶ Arlene Tollman received a suspended sentence for operating a motor vehicle with a blood-alcohol level of more than .10.

Yes, dear reader. I've got bells that jingle jangle jingle and phrases that dangle dingle dangle. In every one of the reports above, a wayward modifier gives the impression that something shocking was going on in our very halls of justice. If you think the structure of those court sentences is rickety, ask yourself what the following TV listings have in common.

The very last blooper I was able to insert in my book *Anguished English* was this one, which appeared in a major TV magazine in 1987: "Yoko Ono will talk about her husband John Lennon, who was killed in an interview with Barbara Walters."

As I was compiling *More Anguished English*, a reader sent me this cracked gem from the *Boston Globe* TV section: "Former hostage Terry Waite talks about five years of confinement in Beirut with Barbara Walters in a specially expanded segment of *20/20* at 10 on Channel 5."

Incredibly, an Associated Press (AP) story that came my way as I was preparing this book included this sentence: "The diving and amateur sports community was in shock Thursday following disclosure by diver Greg Louganis, who speaks freely of his contracting AIDS in a *20/20* interview with Barbara Walters to be broadcast by ABC tonight."

What is it about Barbara Walters, I ask myself, that causes people to dangle their participles in public?

What is it about the American understanding of grammar that causes people to misplace their modifiers so habitually?

The AP carried a feature story on sexual practices in America: "Author Shere Hite wrote that 75 percent of women married more than five years reported having affairs in response to her questionnaire." Let's have a look at that questionnaire!

Celebrating the iron man achievement of Baltimore Orioles shortstop Cal Ripken, a *Washington Times* reporter wrote, "Cal Ripken tied Lou Gehrig's record for playing 2,130 consecutive games against the California Angels." Must have been a two-team league.

The poet and professor James Dickey was guest of honor at "a surprise luncheon with a birthday cake thrown by several close friends in the English Department." With friends like that, who needs enemies?

"There will be a week-long conference for men who experienced incest with speaker Dr. Jarvis at Ranchero Capistrano." I don't recommend Dr. Jarvis.

Here are more of my favorite mangled modifiers:

▶ They gathered in his Queens Road condominium and

sat on the red velvet sofa and the upholstered rocker with carved gooseneck arms that belonged to his mother.

▶ Anna Anderson requested that she be cremated before her death.

▶ Nelson became the 1,919th actor to be honored this week with a star on the Hollywood Walk of Fame.

▶ She danced every night with the captain of the boat in high-heeled shoes.

▶ Through the use of ultrasound, a University of Washington researcher studies women who develop high blood pressure during pregnancy with the assistance of AHA-WA funds.

▶ The blaze was extinguished before any damage was done by the local fire department.

▶ Most of the nation's corporate honchos are white Protestant males, with three kids who have been married to the same stay-at-home woman for 20 years.

▶ Gregory Hartell, Dover Township, is awarded a Purple Heart Medal 41 years after he was injured in the Korean War by George Best, commissioner of the State Veterans Affairs Office.

▶ State Rep. Ira Farrar explains legislation that would restrict abortions in Pennsylvania to members of the state House of Representatives.

▶ I am a single parent with a 2-and-a-half-year-old daughter who has been unable to attend Craig University because of student loans.

▶ The meetings held on Monday and yesterday included presentations by a priest who is a psychiatrist specializing in the diagnosis and treatment of sexual disorders among other experts.

▶ Vice President Gore hobbled up to a small stage filled with Democratic candidates on crutches, having ruptured his Achilles' tendon while playing basketball.

▶ On last Saturday, while driving down East Vance Street, a tree limb fell to the ground along with live wires.

▶ One longtime resident recalled the days when Manhattan Burrough President Mary Slocumb used to stroll around the neighborhood gathering signatures in long skirts.

▶ American Catholic theologians will have to wait and see the exact wording of a French document permitting the use of condoms before engaging in theological debate.

▶ They saw a car sitting on top of a three-foot stone wall up against a tree with a lady in it.

▶ Three tenements on Spring Street were seriously damaged when a man ignited a gas tank that had been removed from a car with his cigarette lighter.

▶ Advil should not be taken if you've ever had a severe allergic reaction to aspirin or any other form of pain reliever without consulting your doctor first.

▶ He provided background information about the life of a man who gained national attention after being mutilated by his wife for the NBC news program *Now* with Tom Brokaw.

▶ After three days of lying in state in Montreal and

Quebec, the high and mighty came to Quebec for Levesque's state funeral at Notre Dame Cathedral.

▶ Sponsored by the Winthrop House, the Beaux Arts Trio will perform Zemlinsky's Trio in D minor, op. 3, Schubert's Trio in E-flat Minor, op. 100, and a work to be announced by Mozart at 8 P.M. in Sanders Theatre.

▶ The senator used the term *the titty bill* in referring to a bill that would ban nude dancing during a discussion with another lawmaker.

▶ Children on school buses weighing less than 10,000 pounds must be restrained.

▶ We will not accept a gift from anyone larger than $5,000.

▶ Do not sweep an area where there have been rodents with a broom.

▶ A Grand Rapids neighborhood is getting some help in fighting crime and protecting children from the city commission.

Typographical Terrors

Great Panty Fillers

Written by the famous Irish poet, Ann O'Nymous, "The Typochondriac" is a popular item in the folk-photocopy and e-mail circuits:

> The typographical error is a slippery thing and sly.
> You can hunt till you are dizzy, but it somehow will
> get by,
> Till the forms are off the presses. It is strange how
> still it sleeps.
> It shrinks down in a corner, and it never stirs or
> peeps.

That typographical error, too small for human eyes,
Till the ink is on the paper, when it grows to mountain size.
The boss just stares with horror, then he grabs his
hair and groans.
The copy reader drops his head upon his hands and
moans.
The remainder of the issue may be clean as clean
can be,
But that typographical error is the only thing you
see.

INJURED? blares the headline of a full-page ad in the "Attorneys" section of the Albuquerque, New Mexico, Yellow Pages. "We Can Help You—Madden, Berkes & Doyle." The three partners go on to promise "24-Hr. Service. Free Consultation. No Fee Until Successful. Proven Results!" But then the Madden, Berkes & Doyle display ends with its Freudian slip showing: "Representing the Seriously Insured."

Ah, the difference a single letter can make.

Writer Max Hall explains, "Some words are more vulnerable to misprinting than others. Consider the word *public*. Proofreaders should give it special attention because its skinny fourth letter has a mysterious tendency to slip away."

Indeed, I receive at least fifty examples of *public*-gone-*pubic* mistakes every year—pubic lectures, pubic beaches, pubic everything. A sign on a city park fence reads, "This pubic area is open to all." A huge front-page headline in a Massachusetts daily newspaper blared, $500 MILLION PLEDGED FOR PUBIC EDUCATION. Typos like these hit below the belt.

A few of the *pubic* submissions marvelously unite topic and typo. A typing error in a letter to *The Miami*

Herald about press coverage of Colorado Senator Gary Hart's amorous escapades with Donna Rice made it read, "Let us not forget that the American press spares no one in pubic life." About Puritan adulterers in the 1660s, a student wrote that they were "branded or pubically punished as an example to others." In an *Atlanta Journal* article headlined JUDGE TAGS FILM OBSCENE, this sentence stood straight out: "A civil suit was filed against the theater by the district attorney, asking the court to declare the movie a pubic nuisance."

The best *pubic* gaffe I've ever received comes from a reader in Fryburg, Maine: "Sexually addicted professionals who have successfully completed comprehensive assessment and primary treatment can usually return to practice without compromising pubic health and safety."

The parade of typos that follows is enough to make anyone a typochondriac:

▶ *An interoffice memo:* Although she is bright, I would not recommend this typo of person for the job.

▶ Representatives of the American Cancer Society will be on campus next Friday to provide instruction on self-examination for signs of cancer. A registered nurse will explain how to look for signs of breast cancer, and another representative will show you how to examine your elf for cancer of the testicles.

▶ OPERA: The Lady of the Camellias travels her tragic path in *La Triviata*, performed by the Davisville Opera Feb. 3 and 5.

▶ Mr. Alfred Dayton, of Lisbon, North Dakota, stopped here en route to Fostoria to say hell to his many friends.

▶ *At the top of a full-page grocery ad:* Great Panty Fillers.

▶ When telephone directors become obsolete, they are usually gathered and sold to waste-paper companies for conversion into pulp and the manufacture of new paper. They are torn in two lengthwise, then chopped into small bits in a powerful machine.

▶ An invitation to a testimonial dinner announces enthusiastically, "We are honored to saute Megan Casey and Brian Cafferty." (Can't we have them lightly fried instead?)

▶ She received a B.A. in International Relations (magna cum laude) at the University of Southern California in 1962 and pursued graduate students at the London School of Economics.

▶ Queens prosecutors will fight the ruling that overturned the conviction of Michael Nussbaum on charges that he helped Donald Manes solicit a bride for the awarding of cable television franchises.

▶ Downtown L.A. has its fair share of buried treasurers.

▶ Self-Realization fellowship is resolved to show you that Comic Consciousness is attainable in one lifetime.

▶ Spend an evening listening to the Boston Poops.

▶ Try Lifebuoy soap for around-the-cock protection.

▶ Suzanne Wiley's gladiola garden has been attracting considerable attention of late. She spends many hours each day in the garden with her large collection of beautiful pants.

▶ Estelle Benzinger, 37, suffered the loss of the tip of the third finger on the right hand when she fell from a moving taxicab Friday night. Police reported that Benzinger was shitting in the back seat of the cab and had been leaning forward conversing with another passenger in the front seat.

▶ According to sources, negotiations between the school board and the teachers is at an impasse. The next step is medication and this cannot be completed in time for any raises to be voted on at the March 3 school meeting.

▶ Dolores Del Rio in the romantic story of *Evangeline*, Henry Wadsworth Longfellow's immoral love epic.

▶ If prime rib is your thing, they have a dull dinner with salad, potato, and beverage.

▶ It took many rabbits many years to write the Talmud.

▶ His Republicans are a couple of dilettantes looking for six years on the public doll.

▶ The victim was taken to the hospital, where his position was undermined.

▶ George Washington's Mike Zargado goes up for an easy shit in Colonials' losing effort against Villanova at Smith Center.

▶ A turdey dinner sponsored by the West Lenoir P.T.A. will be held in the school cafeteria from 4:30 until 7 P.M. Friday.

▶ An estimated 129,000 Americans had returned to the upper Chesapeake Bay this spring to spawn, evidence that the gradual comeback of the ravaged species had resumed after an off-year in 1993.

▶ GIRL. Reliable, wants afternoon work five lays a week.

▶ Weather: Cloudy with a chance of this morning.

▶ Patient complains of pain in humerous other regions. [Like the funny bone?]

▶ Eloise Wilkins was 100 Wednesday, but she had no advice on how to love a century.

▶ "A few years ago an 83-year-old woman I met on a bus told me she was convinced good thoughts and a good disposition provided the foundation for living to a ripe 5d tO," she said.

▶ Defendant was charged with carless driving.

▶ Three bedroom brick ranch, LR with fireplace, new family room with fireplace and large dick.

▶ HELP WANTED: Two part-time Certified Nursing Assistants. P.M. Shit, every other weekend.

▶ Heartworm is an infectious, life-threatening, cardio-vascular disease spread by misquotes.

▶ Homebuyers take a look at the classy new 3 bedrm. 2400 sq. ft. home. Located in nice neighborhood with breeding space.

▶ 27 Acres. Nicely wooded. White bitch and oak.

▶ *From a Vespers liturgy:* Keep us toady, Lord, without sin.

▶ As a result of the explosion, a number of area widows were shattered.

▶ One man was electrocuted when he came in contact with a live wife.

▶ VICTORY IN DSYLEXIA BATTLE

▶ She drives a turk for a construction company.

▶ Dig the ground over thoroughly and then pant.

▶ Question: What will take the wrinkles out of a diplomat?

▶ The children had a turkey raffle in November and some children have participated in the Rend-A-Kid project.

▶ As no payment is forthcoming, we are closing our flies at this time.

▶ ETHIOPIA GETS TWO LOANS; $17.45 TOTAL

▶ CITY ABOLISHES REALITY LICENSE

▶ SWF wanted, 18–25. Attractive and physically fat.

▶ Her partner, Randy Gelo, is one of the Chief Teachers in the Body Works School of Marital Arts.

▶ Following a trip to Mexico, the couple, who met on a blind date set up by a fiend, will live in Waco.

▶ A lumber truck lost part of its load when several broads fell into the middle of Dalton Street.

▶ Replacement Insurance Company. Without it, your lice will never be the same.

▶ As your assemblyman, I will bring real-world experience to Sacramento to fight for lover taxes.

▶ California workers are overworked and underlaid.